REBEL ANGELS

REBEL ANGELS

25 POETS OF THE NEW FORMALISM

Edited by

Mark Jarman & David Mason

Story Line Press

1996

Story Line Press, Three Oaks Farm, Brownsville, OR 97327

This publication was made possible thanks in part to the generous support of the
Nicholas Roerich Museum, the Andrew W. Mellon Foundation, the National
Endowment for the Arts, and our individual contributors.

Book design by Chiquita Babb

Library of Congress Cataloging-in-Publication Data

Rebel angels : 25 poets of the new formalism / edited by Mark Jarman &
   David Mason.
      p. cm.
   ISBN 10885266-33-2 (cloth). — ISBN 1-885266-30-8 (pbk.)
      1. American poetry—20th century. 2. Literary form. I. Jarman,
   Mark. II. Mason, David, 1954–   .
   PS615.R43 1996
   811'.5408—dc20   96-31967
                                                        CIP

For Frederick Morgan

Acknowledgments

Grateful acknowledgment is given to the following:

ELIZABETH ALEXANDER, "Who I Think You Are," "Deadwood Dick," "Letter: Blues," *The Venus Hottentot,* University of Virginia Press, 1990; JULIA ALVAREZ, "How I Learned to Sweep," "33," "Woman's Work," *Homecoming: New & Collected Poems,* NAL/Dutton, 1996; BRUCE BAWER, "View from an Airplane at Night over California," "On Leaving the Artist's Colony," "Grand Central Station, 20 December 1987," *Coast to Coast,* Story Line Press, 1993; RAFAEL CAMPO, "For J.W.," "Aunt Toni's Heart," "Allegory," *The Other Man Was Me,* Arte Publico Press, 1994; "El Día de los Muertos," *The Threepenny Review,* Rafael Campo, 1995; TOM DISCH, "Entropic Villanelle," "The Rapist's Villanelle," "Convalescing in London," Zewhyexary," "A Bookmark," "The Clouds," *Yes, Let's: New and Selected Poems,* Johns Hopkins University Press, 1989; "Ballade of the New God," Tom Disch, 1995; FREDERICK FEIRSTEIN, "The Rune-Maker," *Survivors,* David Lewis, 1974; "Mark Stern Wakes Up," *Manhattan Carnival,* Countryman Press, 1981; "Mark Stern," *City Life,* Story Line Press, 1991; DANA GIOIA, "Lives of the Great Composers," "The Country Wife," *Daily Horoscope,* Graywolf Press, 1985; "Counting the Children," "Guide to the Other Gallery," "Maze Without a Minotaur," "My Confessional Sestina," *The Gods of Winter,* Graywolf Press, 1991; "Summer Storm," Dana Gioia, 1995; EMILY GROSHOLZ, "On the Ferry, Toward Patras," "Remembering the Ardèche," *The River Painter,* Illinois University Press, 1984; "The Old Fisherman," "The Outer Banks," *Shores and Headlands,* Princeton University Press, 1988; "Back Trouble," "Life of a Salesman," "Eden," *Eden,* Johns Hopkins University Press, 1992; R. S. GWYNN, "Among Philistines," "Anacreontic," "The Drive-In," *The Drive-In,* University of Missouri Press, 1986; "Approaching a Significant Birthday, He Peruses *The Norton Anthology of Poetry,*" "Body Bags," *Texas Poets in Concert: A Quartet,* University of North Texas Press, 1990; "The Classroom at the Mall," "Release," *The Area Code of God,* Aralia Press, 1993; MARILYN HACKER, "Wagers," "'Did you love well what very soon you left?,'" *Love, Death and the Changing of the Seasons,* Arbor House, 1986; "Nights of 1964–1966: The Old Reliable, "Rune of the Finland Woman," "Elevens," *Selected Poems: 1965–1990,* Norton, 1994; "Elysian Fields," "Cancer Winter," *Winter Numbers,* Norton, 1995; RACHEL HADAS, "Journey Out," *Slow Transparency,* Wesleyan University Press, 1983; "Three Silences," *Pass It On,* Princeton University Press, 1989; "Moments of Summer," *Crosscurrents,* Rachel Hadas, 1989; "Sentimental Education," *Mirrors of Astonishment,* Rutgers University Press, 1992; "The Red Hat," *The New Yorker,* Rachel Hadas, 1995; ANDREW HUDGINS, "Saints and Strangers," *Saints and Strangers,* Houghton Mifflin, 1985; "The Hereafter," *After the Lost War,* Houghton Mifflin, 1988; "Dead Christ," "Praying Drunk," "Two Ember Days in Alabama,"

The Never-Ending, Houghton Mifflin, 1991; "Elegy for My Father, Who Is Not Dead," "The Telling," *The Glass Hammer*, Houghton Mifflin, 1994; PAUL LAKE, "Crime and Punishment," "Blue Jay," "In Rough Weather," "Introduction to Poetry," *Another Kind of Travel*, University of Chicago Press, 1988; SYDNEY LEA, "The Wrong Way Will Haunt You," *The Floating Candles*, Illinois University Press, 1982; "Telescope," *No Sign*, University of Georgia Press, 1987; "At the Flyfisher's Shack," "Clouded Evening, Late September," *Prayer for the Little City*, Scribners, 1990; "Insomnia: The Distances," "The Feud," *The Blainville Testament*, Story Line Press, 1992; BRAD LEITHAUSER, "The Ghost of a Ghost," *Hundreds of Fireflies*, Knopf, 1982; "Post-Coitum Tristesse: A Sonnet," "The Haunted," *Cats of the Temple*, Knopf, 1986; "Old Bachelor Brother," *The Mail from Anywhere*, Knopf, 1990; PHILLIS LEVIN, "The Shadow Returns," "A Meeting of Friends," "The Lost Bee," "Night Coach," *Temples and Fields*, University of Georgia Press, 1988; CHARLES MARTIN, "Satyr, Cunnilinguent: To Herman Melville," "Sharks at the New York Aquarium," *Room for Error*, University of Georgia Press, 1978; "Speech Against Stone," "Metaphor of Grass in California," "E.S.L.," "Easter Sunday, 1985," *Steal the Bacon*, Johns Hopkins University Press, 1987; "Victoria's Secret," *Hellas*, Charles Martin, 1994; MARILYN NELSON, "Balance," "Chopin," "The Ballad of Aunt Geneva," *The Homeplace*, Louisiana State University Press, 1990; MOLLY PEACOCK, "Desire," "Those Paperweights with Snow Inside," *Raw Heaven*, Random House, 1984; "How I Come to You," "Dream Come True," *Take Heart*, Random House, 1989; "The Wheel," "Have You Ever Faked an Orgasm?," "The Return," *Original Love*, Norton, 1995; WYATT PRUNTY, "A Winter's Tale," "Insomnia," *What Women Know, What Men Believe*, Johns Hopkins University Press, 1986; "To Be Sung on the Fourth of July," *Balance as Belief*, Johns Hopkins University Press, 1989; "The Ferris Wheel," "Elderly Lady Crossing on Green," "A Note of Thanks," *The Run of the House*, Johns Hopkins University Press, 1993; "Reading Before We Read: Horoscope and Weather," Wyatt Prunty, 1995; MARY JO SALTER, "Welcome to Hiroshima," *Henry Purcell in Japan*, Knopf, 1985; "Summer 1983," *Unfinished Painting*, Knopf, 1989; "What Do Women Want?," "Frost at Midnight," *Sunday Skaters*, Knopf, 1994; TIMOTHY STEELE, "Eros," "The Library," "Joseph," *The Color Wheel*, Johns Hopkins University Press, 1994; "The Wartburg, 1521–22," "In The King's Rooms," "Timothy," "An Aubade," *Sapphics and Uncertainities: Poems, 1970–1986*, The University of Arkansas Press, 1995; FREDERICK TURNER, "Spring Evening," "April Wind," "On the Pains of Translating Miklós Radnóti," *April Wind*, University of Virginia, 1991; RACHEL WETZSTEON, "Three Songs," "Three Songs," "Dinner at Le Caprice," *The Other Stars*, Penguin Books, 1994; GREG WILLIAMSON, "Walter Parmer," "The Counterfeiter," "Waterfall," "Annual Returns," *The Silent Partner*, Story Line Press, 1995.

Contents

Rachel Wetzsteon

Greg Williamson

Revolution, as the critic Monroe Spears has observed, is bred in the bone of the American character. That character has been manifest in modern American poetry in particular. So it is no surprise that the most significant development in recent American poetry has been a resurgence of meter and rhyme, as well as narrative, among large numbers of younger poets, after a period when these essential elements of verse had been suppressed. We hope to demonstrate that the poets known as the New Formalists have produced poems deserving attention for the beauty, accuracy, and memorability of their language, as well as their feeling and ideas. This anthology aims to entertain, but also to instruct by gathering the best work of twenty-five important new poets who write in a wide variety of forms—some traditional, some newly-minted—out of the experience of their generation. These poets represent nothing less than a revolution, a fundamental change, in the art of poetry as it is practiced in this country.

The poets collected here were all born since 1940. They came of age as writers at a time when meter and rhyme had largely been abandoned by American poets. The cultural upheavals of the 1960's and '70's, coming on the heels of modernism and two World Wars, produced a poetry in which traditional measures were thought to be antithetical to truth. The flourishing of free verse during the Cold War was itself a change, a revolution bred by the American character. Younger poets at that time read the work of Allen Ginsberg, Amiri Baraka, Diane Wakoski, Denise Levertov, and studied the shift in style from formal to free verse in poets like Robert Lowell and Adrienne Rich. Very often the result, as they imitated their elders, was a poetry that spoke to social concerns, but did so in a language of narrowing formal range. Poetry and prose became nearly indistinguishable, and "verse" a pejorative term. The alliterative heritage and bountiful vocabulary of English suffered, too, as the aural range of poetry shrank to the plainest diction possible.

Of course there were older American poets who never abandoned traditional forms, and some were teachers who kept older aesthetic values alive, withstanding attacks on their own work by critics who believed that measure was un-American. One thinks of J. V. Cunningham, Anthony

Hecht, Howard Nemerov, and Richard Wilbur, along with X. J. Kennedy and Mona Van Duyn, whose magazines *Counter/Measures* and *Perspective* remained friendly to writers of verse. One recalls that Donald Justice, who had abandoned the meters of his early work, returned to them in the mid-70's. These poets were courageous in their commitment to their art. But they were also, when young, trained in that art and immersed in the formal aesthetic of Yvor Winters, John Crowe Ransom, Allen Tate, and the New Critics. They were inspired by what might be called "the high canon of literature," bred from English Renaissance ideas of art, irony, and decorum.

Though acknowledging their debt to these older masters, the New Formalists have largely different roots. These younger poets grew up in the era of rock music, the Viet Nam War, the Civil Rights Movement, birth control, drugs, and feminism. Not only was the America they inhabited radically different from that of the '30's and '40's, when many of their teachers came of age, but the literature that surrounded them had few ties to tradition. The very word "tradition" became routinely associated with some of T. S. Eliot's personal views, and was dismissed out of hand as anathema. Younger poets were schooled to be unschooled. Learning and artifice were regarded as politically suspect matters. American poetry had entered another romantic phase, like a late adolescence.

What is remarkable is not so much that a few older poets stood their ground before this onslaught, but that younger writers across the political, cultural, and racial spectrum began to turn away from the dominant literary trends. Out of need and affection, they rediscovered the inherent power of measured speech, even rhyme, and the power of narrative to convey experience, including minority or marginalized experience. They understood as well that an entire realm of pleasure was being denied to them by much contemporary poetry. Some of these younger poets were taught by Robert Fitzgerald and Elizabeth Bishop at Harvard, Yvor Winters and Donald Davie at Stanford, Allen Tate at Sewanee, John Hollander at Yale, and J. V. Cunningham at Brandeis. But a great many younger poets wholly without the advantage of such training sought out information about meter where they could, instinctively feeling that techniques common to popular music, for example, still had valid uses in poetry.

The critic Robert McPhillips has observed that early volumes of poetry by Charles Martin, Timothy Steele, and others went largely unnoticed. By the late 1970's there were few critics who could see what was happening, or could understand why a younger generation of poets would feel limited by the kinds of free verse most commonly published. McPhillips suggests that it was the publication of Brad Leithauser's debut volume, *Hundreds of Fireflies* (1982), that first drew major attention to the new trend. That may be true, and by the mid-80's there were anthologies like *Strong Measures,* edited by Philip Dacey and David Jauss, and *Ecstatic Occasions, Expedient Forms,* edited by David Lehman, to signal this new interest in meter. The first of these was too catholic in its definition of form to be of lasting use to teachers, and both books lumped older and younger poets together, blurring the distinctions between generations. Our anthology is more precisely defined in both formal and historical terms.

The term New Formalism, originally used as a dismissive epithet by critics hostile to the movement, is usually thought inadequate even by its adherents. Some poets like Frederick Turner and Frederick Feirstein found the term Expansive Poetry more to their liking, because it could include the related phenomenon of New Narrative poems, many of which are also composed in meter. The New Narrative, supported by journals like *The Hudson Review, The New England Review,* and *The Reaper,* has introduced a new kind of realism to contemporary poetry, influenced by Robinson, Frost, and Jeffers, but also by the whole range of modern fiction. The Calcutta-born poet Vikram Seth (partly educated in California, but now returned to his native India) published *The Golden Gate* (1986), a novel about twenty-something San Franciscans written in an elaborately-rhymed stanza borrowed from Pushkin. Julia Alvarez has written a fictionalized autobiography in the form of a sonnet sequence, "33." Andrew Hudgins' *After the Lost War* is a fresh, book-length treatment of the Civil War and its aftermath. This is to say nothing of a range of narratives by Dana Gioia, Paul Lake, Robert McDowell, and Mary Jo Salter, or the experiments in verse drama by Tom Disch.

We choose to retain the term New Formalism, however, because it best describes this movement and the distinction between free and formal verse. It is understood that a formalist writes primarily in the meters of the English tradition and often in the verse forms associated with those meters. That is the case with the poets gathered here. But the New Formalism also reflects trends of broad cultural significance, not unrelated to the return of melody in serious music, representation in the visual arts, and character and plot in fiction. The neglect of the maker's art in poetry resulted in a literary climate in which, for the first time in history, the artist's personal life and the correctness of his or her political attitudes became important aesthetic criteria. It is also true that hardly any significant new literary critics other than the feminists appeared among poets in the 1960's and '70's. As the New Formalists have taken on the responsibility of cogent criticism, the outlines of this new movement have become clearer. While the wide-scale abandonment of traditional forms—and whole genres like satirical, narrative, and dramatic verse—has proven too limiting, popular phenomena as diverse as cowboy poetry and rap music demonstrate that the rhyme and meter that characterize Emily Dickinson are just as American as the free verse of Walt Whitman.

One of the most notorious attacks upon poets who have the effrontery to use rhyme and meter was Diane Wakoski's essay, "The New Conservatism in American Poetry" (*American Book Review,* May–June 1986), which denounced poets as diverse as John Hollander, Robert Pinsky, T. S. Eliot, and Robert Frost for using techniques Wakoski considered Eurocentric. She is particularly incensed with younger poets writing in measure. Conflating political and aesthetic agendas, she refers to "this new generation coming along which cannot deal with anxiety of any sort and thus wants a secure set of formulas and rules, whether it be for verse forms or for how to cure the national deficit." The problem with pronouncements like Wakoski's is that they obscure any useful aesthetic distinctions. In this case, she actually refers to Hollander as "Satan." Wakoski talks about "a Whitman tradition" and William Carlos Williams' search for a "new measure," but expects her readers to take these vague ramblings on faith, never making it clear why Frost and Pinsky are any less American as poets, and never coming to grips with the contradictions in Williams' theories. Her essay is the verbal equivalent of flailing arms.

Rejecting the sentimental notion that meter is un-American, New Formalists have contributed to a new consensus, defending the material value of verse against the encroachment of prose, while simultaneously defending popular subjects against the charge of philistinism. These are, after all, poets who came of age when television was the most powerful medium. Ultimately, though, the rediscovery of meter by younger writers reminds us that language requires renewal by each succeeding generation.

The act of making poems in measured speech assumes a valued civility, putting a premium not only on technique, but also on a larger cultural vision that restores harmony and balance to the arts—an idea of great importance in critical books like Frederick Turner's *Natural Classicism,* Dana Gioia's *Can Poetry Matter?,* and Bruce Bawer's *Prophets and Professors.* As Timothy Steele has written in his scholarly treatise, *Missing Measures: Modern Poetry and the Revolt Against Meter:*

> What is essential to human life and to its continuance remains a love of nature, an enthusiasm for justice, a readiness of good humor, a spontaneous susceptibility to beauty and joy, an interest in our past, a hope for our future, and, above all, a desire that others should have the opportunity and encouragement to share these qualities. An art of measured speech nourishes these qualities in a way no other pursuit can.

A new generation of American poets was bound to discover this aesthetic common ground despite their varied social and political backgrounds. Our anthology will demonstrate this variety. The New Formalism unites poets as different as Marilyn Hacker and Sydney Lea, Rafael Campo and R. S. Gwynn, poets who are chatty and elegiac, satirical and gently moving. Their range of subjects and forms has already done much to restore vitality to the art. Our anthology marks this flowering and gathers these individual poets together between covers for the first time. These twenty-five writers are among those who will lead American poetry into the 21st century.

The editors of this volume have set several criteria for inclusion. First, we gathered only American poets born in 1940 or later, who came of age as writers in the 1970's, '80's, and '90's, and are still developing their art. As we revised this anthology, we left out many fine poets, some for reasons as arbitrary as citizenship, others because they had not yet published a book. Second, we chose only poems in which the use of form was rigorous and commanding. New Formalist poets have not always been strict adherents of accentual-syllabic meter. Some use syllabics or accentual meters. Some of the poems collected here are experimental in their meter, but we did want confidence in both line and rhetoric. There are no "pseudo-formal" poems, to use Dana Gioia's term. Third, we wanted no poems that were merely formal. That is, poems that were sound exercises in prosody, but did not move or convince us in human terms, were excluded.

It has been a challenge to choose examples from some poets' work. Some have done their best writing in book-length sequences and narratives. We have tried to excerpt where possible or to choose shorter, more self-contained poems. Finally, we wanted to include the work of several newer poets with at least one book in print, along with poets who were better known. This suggests that the New Formalism as a movement has not been a narrow one, but has continued to attract new adherents from many backgrounds. The question of omission from and inclusion in anthologies is always imperfectly addressed, and ours is no exception. Readers can find suggestions for further reading in the back of this volume.

If we make a special claim for the New Formalists, it is that there is more variety in their approach to form and subject than in some work of previous generations. At times in their work we see fluent elegance and skill, at others a vital roughness. In their poems there is an audible discovery of something lost, a sense of recasting from scrap, of reinventing the wheel, of new forms exploding from old ones. As Americans, these poets share a love of the unliterary. They find their subjects disguised in unlikelihood. Because they are formalists, they give a new vernacular life to ancient forms, but they also invent new forms of their own. Surely this is a function of that innate revolutionary bred into the American character. Whenever a fundamental change has taken place, and old, discarded forms have been rediscovered, their revival will include a reconfiguration. In the hands of these poets, traditional forms like blank verse and the sonnet, while still conforming to their ancient rules, seem brand new.

Readers who take pleasure in form, or who want a map to guide them through the shifting and variable and endlessly fascinating landscape of contemporary American poetry, will find joyful illumination in the poems that follow.

REBEL ANGELS

WHO I THINK YOU ARE

Empty out your pockets nighttime, Daddy.
Keys and pennies, pocket watch, a favored
photograph of Ma, and orange-flavored
sucker-candies, in the dresser caddy.

Grandpa leaves his silver in his trousers,
potions for catarrh set on the bureau,
and his Castile soap, "All Pure." Oh,
those oval, olive cakes for early rousers!

Baba's home is different from my daddy's:
the sofa arms are draped with quiet lace,
Does he fix fish with cardamon and mace?
Coupons in a cookie tin. Meat patties,

Steaming Cream of Wheat and ripe banana,
juice cups with the little paper hats
the guava jelly jars on plastic mats.
We are your children and receive your manna.

I see you both. I see what's in your pockets.
Coins from you, Dad'. Baba? What's for me?
Fortune cookies, child, and sacks of tea,
cigar bands and glinting, dimestore lockets.

DEADWOOD DICK

> "Come on and slant your eyes again, O
> Buffalo Bill."
> —*Carl Sandburg*

Colored cowboy named Nat Love,
They called him Deadwood Dick.
A black thatch of snakes for hair,
Close-mouthed. Bullet-hipped.

One knee bent like his rifle butt,
Just so. Rope. Saddle. Fringe.
Knock this white boy off my shoulder.
Stone-jawed, cheekboned man.

Mama, there are black cowboys.
A fistful of black crotch.
Deadwood Dick: Don't fuck with me.
Black cowboy. Leather hat.

LETTER: BLUES

> "Those Great Lake Winds
> blow all around:
> I'm a light-coat man
> in a heavy-coat town."
>
> —*Waring Cuney*

Yellow freesia arc like twining arms;
I'm buying shower curtains, smoke alarms,
And Washington, and you, Love—states away.
The clouds are flat. The sky is going grey.

I'm fiddling with the juice jug, honey pot,
White chrysanthemums that I just bought.
At home, there is a violet, 3-D moon
And pachysandra vines for me to prune,

And old men with checkered shirts, suspenders,
Paper bags and Cutty bottles, menders
Of frayed things and balding summer lawns,
Watching TV baseball, shelling prawns.

The women that we love! Their slit-eyed ways
Of telling us to mind, pop-eyed dismays.
We need these folks, each one of them. We do.
The insides of my wrists still ache with you.

Does the South watch over wandering ones
Under different moons and different suns?
I have my mother's copper ramekin,
A cigar box to keep your letters in.

At least the swirl ceilings are very high,
And the Super's rummy, sort of sly.
I saw a slate-branched tree sway from the roots—
I've got to buy some proper, winter boots.

So many boxes! Crates and crates of books.
I must get oil soap, bleach, and picture hooks.
A sidewalk crack in Washington, D.C.
Will feed my city dirt roots. Wait for me.

HOW I LEARNED TO SWEEP

My mother never taught me sweeping. . . .
One afternoon she found me watching
t.v. She eyed the dusty floor
boldly, and put a broom before
me, and said she'd like to be able
to eat her dinner off that table,
and nodded at my feet, then left.
I knew right off what she expected
and went at it. I stepped and swept;
the t.v. blared the news; I kept
my mind on what I had to do,
until in minutes, I was through.
Her floor was as immaculate
as a just-washed dinner plate.
I waited for her to return
and turned to watch the President,
live from the White House, talk of war:
in the Far East our soldiers were
landing in their helicopters
into jungles their propellers
swept like weeds seen underwater
while perplexing shots were fired
from those beautiful green gardens
into which these dragonflies
filled with little men descended.
I got up and swept again
as they fell out of the sky.
I swept all the harder when
I watched a dozen of them die. . .
as if their dust fell through the screen

upon the floor I had just cleaned.
She came back and turned the dial;
the screen went dark. *That's beautiful,*
she said, and ran her clean hand through
my hair, and on, over the window-
sill, coffee table, rocker, desk,
and held it up—I held my breath—
That's beautiful, she said, impressed,
she hadn't found a speck of death.

WOMAN'S WORK

Who says a woman's work isn't high art?
She'd challenge as she scrubbed the bathroom tiles.
Keep house as if the address were your heart.

We'd clean the whole upstairs before we'd start
downstairs. I'd sigh, hearing my friends outside.
Doing her woman's work was a hard art

to practice when the summer sun would bar
the floor I swept till she was satisfied.
She kept me prisoner in her housebound heart.

She'd shine the tines of forks, the wheels of carts,
cut lacy lattices for all her pies.
Her woman's work was nothing less than art.

And, I, her masterpiece since I was smart,
was primed, praised, polished, scolded and advised
to keep a house much better than my heart.

I did not want to be her counterpart!
I struck out . . . but became my mother's child:
a woman working at home on her art,
housekeeping paper as if it were her heart.

from 33

Where are the girls who were beautiful?
I don't mean back in the olden days either,
I mean yesterday and the day before
yesterday? Tell me, if you can, where will
I find breathless Vivien or Marilyn,
her skirt blown up? Certainly Natalie,
struggling in the cold waves, deserved to be
fished out when the crew finished and given
her monogrammed beach towel and a hot drink.
How many times didn't we pay good money
to see them saved from worse catastrophes
as they trembled in swimsuits on the brink
of death, Rita and Jean, Lana and Joan,
Frances, Marlene—their names sound like our own.

◆

The women on my mother's side were known
for beauty and were given lovely names
passed down for generations. I knew them
as my pretty aunts: Laura, who could turn
any head once, and Anna, whose husband
was so devoted he would lay his hand-
kerchief on seats for her and when she rose
thanked her; there was Rosa, who got divorced
twice, her dark eyes and thick hair were to blame;
and my mother Julia, who was a catch
and looks it in her wedding photographs.
My sister got her looks, I got her name,
and its suits me that between resemblance
and words, I got the right inheritance.

◆

Get yourself something in our name you need,
Sounds wistful, sounds like they already know
their daughter's life is turbulent, and so
to make up for it, here's pocket money!
Oh God, they think, watching the sad rain fall
from their Munich hotel the afternoon
of my birthday, Why did we bring children
into a world we can't make heads or tails
or sense out of? Perhaps they're visiting
monuments to man's inhumanity
to man, and she turns to him asking simply
Why? And for comfort they hold hands wandering
where thousands died. And I want suddenly
to give them something, anything, they need.

◆

HE: Age doesn't matter when you're both in love!
SHE: You say that now, wait till you've had enough.
HE: I love for keeps. I'll never let you down.
SHE: You lie, my dear, you'll lay me in the ground.
HE: Statistics say I'll probably die first.
SHE: Statistics say most couples get divorced.
HE: Better to love and lose than not at all.
SHE: Better to read the writing on the wall!
HE: You go by loss, you might as well not live.
SHE: Or live, single, and psychoanalyzed.
HE: It breaks my heart to hear you talk that way.
SHE: (Boy in her arms, wiping his tears away,
prescribes the cure for existential ache)
Come in, my sweet, and have some birthday cake.

THE VIEW FROM AN AIRPLANE AT NIGHT, OVER CALIFORNIA

This is a sight that Wordsworth never knew,
whether looking down from mountain, bridge, or hill:
An endless field of lights, white, orange, and blue,
as small and bright as stars, and nearly still,
but moving slowly, many miles below,
in blackness, as stars crawl across the skies,
and ranked in rows that stars will never know,
like beads strung on a thousand latticed ties.
Would even Wordsworth, seeing what I see,
know that these lights are not well-ordered stars
that have been here a near-eternity,
but houses, streetlamps, factories, and cars?
Or has this slim craft made too high a leap
above it all, and is the dark too deep?

ON LEAVING THE ARTISTS' COLONY

The way love rests upon coincidence,
the way a sense of family and home
can flow now, like a stream, through several hearts
transplanted from their diverse native climes
by strangers' choices, violates all sense.

If we had all been here at different times,
I know we'd have formed other loyalties,
drawn other eyes and written other poems,
and I know there are friendships I'd have made
with people whom I now may never meet.

But so be it. Heard melodies are sweet,
and unheard melodies are never played
except on the harmonium of art.
This place we love reminds us how immense
the world is, and how small our cherished part,

and why we feel drawn on toward mysteries,
compelled to paint and sculpt, compose and write.
To think of those who'll be here three months hence,
who'll feel just as we do, and find it hard
believing that emotions so intense

can be so commonplace, is to regard
those mysteries as if with second sight.
It is to sense an elemental rhyme
of soul and soul, to feel a river flow
between our hearts and those we'll never know.

GRAND CENTRAL STATION,
20 DECEMBER 1987

In memoriam M.J.G.

The clock's so huge you can watch the minute hand
crawl steadily toward three. It's after one
on a gray and drizzly Sunday afternoon
before Christmas, and all around me stand

handsome young men who look like paradigms
of American youth. Poised, affluent, and clean-
cut in sweaters that read *Princeton* and *Penn,*
they chat idly, glancing from time to time

at their luggage, and at the clock; they're on
their way to Westport, Mahopac, and Rye,
to houses set beneath a still blue sky,
each with its Porsche, its wide and quiet lawn,

its complement of trees—elm, maple, birch—
and to an exurban sense of harmony
synonymous, for them, with home. And me?
I'm going to a Hastings-on-Hudson church

to say farewell to one who should have been,
sixteen years hence, a freshman Ivy Leaguer
heading home for Christmas—bright, slim, eager
to see his parents, waiting for a train.

FOR J. W.

I know exactly what I want to say,
Except we're men. Except it's poetry,
And poetry is too precise. You know
That when we met on Robert's porch, I knew.
My paper plate seemed suddenly too small;

I stepped on a potato chip. I watched
The ordinary spectacle of birds
Become magnificent until the sky,
Which was an ordinary sky, was blue
And comforting across my face. At least

I thought I knew. I thought I'd seen your face
In poetry, in shapeless clouds, in ice—
Like staring deeply into frozen lakes.
I thought I'd heard your voice inside my chest,
And it was comforting, magnificent,

Like poetry but more precise. I knew,
Or thought I knew, exactly how I felt.
About the insects fizzing in the lawn.
About the stupid, ordinary birds,
About the poetry of Robert Frost,

Fragility and paper plates. I look at you.
Because we're men, and frozen hard as ice—
So hard from muscles spreading out our chests—
I want to comfort you, and say it all.
Except my poetry is imprecise.

AUNT TONI'S HEART

A motorcycle roaring in the distance—
I sigh myself. I loved her. More than Christmas,
Even more than summer. The day before
Another family reunion, chairs
Unfolded on the lawn, like stiff fawns. Thighs
Appeared, veined watermelons—each goodbye
An afternoon of sticky kisses, sweets—

Parked cars made silver rivers from the streets.
I'd hide beneath the table where the men
Played poker in the smoky shade. They bent
Their cards. Red wine, cigars and pepperoni.
It wasn't really whispers when Aunt Toni
Sat right down beside my Uncle Joe—surprise
Is more like it—and stared into his eyes:

She smiled at him, waiting to be dealt
A hand. I remember how the green felt
Seemed perfect, slipped back, like a perfect shrine.
My family grew way outside the lines.
My grandmother would say how hard it was
For them when they arrived, each city bus
Gigantic as America, New York

Entire countries warring over work.
They hated Catholics back then, they did.
Italians too. She slowly shook her head.
"That's why you need your family," she'd say.
"Who else is gonna love you?" Which is why

I understood about Aunt Toni's heart.
My grandmother explained that it was hurt—

No, not hurt exactly, just *different*—
And that inside it was an angel sent
When she was small. The angel's name was Love,
And she was lost. "Aunt Toni's old enough
To try to find her angel now—that's all
You need to know. The rest is miracle."
I trailed Aunt Toni all day long: she fed

Me chocolate kisses from her hand. I begged
Her, catching fireflies that night, to show
Her angel-heart to me, but she said no.
My parents still won't talk about the year
Aunt Toni brought Charlene with her, blond hair
Drawn back beneath their helmets, the wind and sun
Greedy for more gold. By then, I'd begun

To see the beauty in the world. I knew
She'd found her angel. My own heart felt new.

ALLEGORY

Outside somewhere, beneath an atmosphere
So pure and new each breath is musical
And silent, mouth-watering, without taste,
So full of butterflies one can't imagine
Because it hurts to be so free, out there

There was a hospital where AIDS was cured
With Chinese cucumbers and royal jelly,
With herbal medicines, vaccines, colostrum.
I went there in a submarine, through space
It seemed, and I was armed with nuclear

ICBMS. I read *The New York Times,*
That's how relaxed and skeptical I was;
I sat upon the floor, my back against
The gleaming missiles. Strangely, no one else
But me was on the submarine, except

The President, whom I'd confined beneath
The lowest deck, inside somewhere where air
Was scarce and hardly breathable. One can't
Imagine what it's like to see a world
Like theirs from such a distance for the first

Time: God, was it beautiful, butterflies
And silent musical wind, the hospital
Where no one paid. I tried to give them small
Pox, missiles, blankets; they looked at me
Like I was crazy, and they asked me why

The President had been incarcerated.
There's no explaining of morality
To savages, I thought. And though it hurt
To leave, to conquer them and take with me
The royal jelly and colostrum, when I aimed

My missiles at their hospital I felt
Much better. Munching on a cucumber,
The light of the explosion brightening
My face, I couldn't help the tears, I was
So sad and happy, all at once, again.

EL DÍA DE LOS MUERTOS

In Mexico, I met myself one day
Along the side of someone's private road.
I recognized the longing in my face.
I felt the heavy burden of the load
I carried. Mexico, I thought, was strange
And very dry. The private road belonged
To friends more powerful than I, enraged
But noble people who like me sang songs
In honor of the dead. In Mexico,
Tradition is as heavy as the sun.
I stared into my eyes. Some years ago,
I told myself, I met a handsome man
Who thought that I was Mexican. The weight
Of some enormous pain, unspeakable
Yet plain, was in his eyes; his shirt was white,
So white it blinded me. After it all
Became more clear, and we were making love
Beneath the cool sheet of the moon, I knew
We were alive. The tiny stars above
Seemed strange and very far. A dry wind blew.
I gave myself to him, and then I asked
Respectfully if I might touch his face.
I did not want to die. His love unmasked,
I saw that I had slept not with disgrace
But with desire. Along the desert road,
A cactus bloomed. As water filled my eyes,
I sang a song in honor of the dead.
They came for me. My grief was like a vise,
And in my blood I felt the virus teem.
My noble friends abandoned me beside

The road. The sun, awakened from its dream,
Rose suddenly. I watched it as I died,
And felt the heaviness of all its gold.
I listened for the singing in the distance.
A man walked toward me. The story he told
Seemed so familiar, pained, and so insistent,
I wished I would live long enough to hear
Its end. This man was very kind to me.
He kissed me, gave me water, held me near.
In Mexico, they sing so beautifully.

ENTROPIC VILLANELLE

Things break down in different ways.
  The odds say croupiers will win.
We can't for that, omit their praise.

I have had heartburn several days,
  And it's ten years since I've been thin.
Things break down in different ways.

Green is the lea and smooth as baize
  Where witless sheep crop jessamine
(We can't, for that, omit their praise),

And meanwhile melanomas graze
  Upon the meadows of the skin
(Things break down in different ways).

Though apples spoil, and meat decays,
  And teeth erode like aspirin,
We can't, for that, omit their praise.

The odds still favor croupiers,
  But give the wheel another spin.
Things break down in different ways:
We can't, for that, omit their praise.

THE RAPIST'S VILLANELLE

She spent her money with such perfect style
The clerks would gasp at each new thing she'd choose.
I couldn't help myself: I had to smile

Or burst. Her slender purse was crocodile,
Her blouse was from Bendel's, as were her shoes.
She spent her money with such perfect style!

I loved her so! She shopped—and all the while
My soul that bustling image would perfuse.
I couldn't help myself: I had to smile

At her hand-knitted sweater from the Isle
Of Skye, an après-skis of bold chartreuse.
She spent her money with such perfect style.

Enchanted by her, mile on weary mile
I tracked my darling down the avenues.
I couldn't help myself. I had to smile

At how she never once surmised my guile.
My heart was hers—I'd nothing else to lose.
She spent her money with such perfect style
I couldn't help myself. I had to smile.

CONVALESCING IN LONDON

Like a drunk treading on his trouser cuffs,
Time lurches past. Time goes too fast.
    I don't know what to do
And lie awake in the dark, overheated room,
    Listening, listening to
Time lurch past. Time goes too fast.

I may not move about too much, nor drink,
My doctors say. I went to the Tower today,
    Where many famous men
And women, waiting to die, found good things to say
    About death (a friend). Then
A few bridges and Hyde Park. Now it is dark.

Since my hepatitis I'm afraid
I've not been entertaining. It's too hot
    In here but when I raise
The window rain comes in, and noises
    From the street. I cannot
Concentrate on anything, except the clock, ticking.

ZEWHYEXARY

Z is the Zenith from which we decline,
While Y is your Yelp as you're twisting your spine.
X is for Xmas; the alternative
Is an X-ray that gives you just one year to live.
So three cheers for Santa, and onward to W.
W's Worry, but don't let it trouble you:
W easily might have been Worse.
V, unavoidably, has to be Verse.
U is Uncertainty. T is a Trial
At which every objection is met with denial.
S is a Sentence of "Guilty as Charged."
R is a Russian whose nose is enlarged
By inveterate drinking, while Q is the Quiet
That falls on a neighborhood after a riot.
P is a Pauper with nary a hope
Of lining his pockets or learning to cope.
O is an Organ transplanted in vain,
While N is the Number of "Enemies Slain':
Three thousand three hundred and seventy-three.
If no one else wants it, could M be for Me?
No, M is reserved for a mad Millionaire,
And L is his Likewise, and goes to his heir.
K is a Kick in the seat of your pants,
And J is the Jury whose gross ignorance
Guaranteed the debacle referred to above.
I's the Inevitability of
Continued inflation and runaway crime,
So draw out your savings and have a good time.
H is your Heart at the moment it breaks,
And G is the Guile it initially takes

To pretend to believe that it someday will heal.
F is the strange Fascination we feel
For whatever's Evil—Yes, Evil is E—
And D is our Dread at the sight of a C,
Which is Corpse, as you've surely foreseen. B is bone.
A could be anything. A is unknown.

A BOOKMARK

Four years ago I started reading Proust.
Although I'm past the halfway point, I still
Have seven hundred pages of reduced
Type left before I reach the end. I will
Slog through. It can't get much more dull than what
Is happening now: he's buying crepe de chine
Wraps and a real, well-documented hat
For his imaginary Albertine.
Oh, what a slimy sort he must have been—
So weak, so sweetly poisonous, so fey!
Four years ago, by God!—and even then
How I was looking forward to the day
I would be able to forgive, at last,
And to forget *Remembrance of Things Past*.

THE CLOUDS

> Do you see yonder cloud that's almost in
> Shape of a camel? *By the mass, and 'tis*
> *Like a camel, indeed.* Methinks it is like
> A weasel. *It is backed like a weasel.*
> Or like a whale? *Very like a whale.*
> Then I will come to my mother by and by.

Coral and shells are heaped until it seems
That everyone is rich, until the dreams
Of millionaires are clothing for the poor;
The world appears as it appeared before
The age of iron or the age of bronze:
Silvery beaches and wide, golden lawns.

Above all, changing: Perfect lambs one moment,
Moses the next, hurling his decalogues.
Elaborate as the handle of a silver spoon
Endlessly lifted to the perplexity
Of your smile. Smiling, collapsing—soundlessly
Offering themselves and moving off.

Slowly they graze the mountaintops, slow
Cows wandering home to their sunset—
Mildly anxious, leaking drops of milk
Into the monumental snow.
Now it is dark. Instead of bells, a blare
Of traffic and the chink of silverware.

A mother, fecund as Tuscany, pleased
To represent something so basically human
That even city people offer it
The yearly tribute of a Christmas card;

And yet she wonders who she'll want to be
Tomorrow when her babies disappear.

Love, you say—you love me. Then you become
A patch of sunlight propped against a wall,
A warmth that vanishes by three o'clock,
A pattern scratched upon a pretty stone,
A thought, a Romanesque basilica
With turgid fables flaking from the dome.

Or words—crisp unambiguous nouns, and verbs
Passing before us at an even pace,
Unswerving, with an army's iron grace;
But lovelier than these, if less distinct,
Those adjectives that decorate a blank,
White, wide, and slightly terrified face.

A wound, perhaps, but I've forgotten it
As if it were a dream that had recurred
Throughout my childhood: something orange, or red;
A flower, or a terrible mistake;
Someone at a previous address
Who gave me mittens, or who gave me socks.

An inclined plane, a wheel, a water glass—
Half engineering, half a work of art;
A human orrery that duplicates
The simple motions of the lungs and heart.
But turn it upside down and it becomes
Confetti circling in a paperweight.

As food flows into them, inaudible
To us, in cadenced shrills, they signal each
To each: I breathe, I move away, I need.
I need. The plankton, every molecule
Of water and of air is shaken by
The swelling and subsiding of their talk.

From century to century, the gist,
The motive antecedent to the act,
The indecipherable sense of it,
Even this, slips; the serried surfaces
Are left, draperies for archaeologists
To number and, provisionally, name.

You: you are the cloud I never name,
The language that I cannot learn, the game,
I neither lose nor altogether win;
Illusion of another world above
The world beneath, outside the world within.
I squint, I blink—but still I see you, love.

BALLADE OF THE NEW GOD

I have decided I'm divine.
Caligula and Nero knew
A godliness akin to mine,
But they are strictly hitherto.
They're dead, and what can dead gods do?
I'm here and now. I'm dynamite.
I'd worship me if I were you.
A new religion starts tonight!

No booze, no pot, no sex, no swine:
I have decreed them all taboo.
My words will be your only wine,
The thought of me your honeydew.
All other thoughts you will eschew.
You'll call yourself a Thomasite
And hymn my praise with loud yahoo.
A new religion starts tonight.

But (you might think) that's asinine!
I'm just as much a god as you.
You may have built yourself a shrine,
But I won't bend my knee. Who
Asked you to be my god? I do,
Who am, as god, divinely right.
Now you must join my retinue:
A new religion starts tonight.

All that I have said is true.
I'm god and you're my acolyte.
Surrender's bliss. I envy you.
A new religion starts tonight.

THE RUNE-MAKER

> "A piece of bone, found at Trondhjem in 1901 with the
> following runic inscription (about A.D. 1050) cut on it:
> 'I loved her as a maiden; I will not trouble Erlend's
> detestable wife; better she should be a widow.'"
> *(Quoted by A.D. Hope for his poem "Meditation On A Bone")*

This bone once moved a hand
That smuggled from my bed
Speechless contraband.
I found where she was led.
She printed on the sand
Her buttocks and her head.

This bone beckoned slaves
That fed her honeyed bread,
Liquor that she craves
Curled on a gluttinous bed.
Like a strumpet she behaves,
Now that her keeper's dead.

The sky turned dark, until
Rain overflowed their gourds.
The startled birds stood still
The palm-leaves flashed like swords.
I felt her body thrill
When I pared away her lord's.

She made my mast unfurl:
She offered me his rut.
But I made his thief's flesh curl
And in this bone I cut:
"I loved her as a girl,
Not as Erlend's slut."

MARK STERN WAKES UP

"Get up!" "Marlene?" I smell the April rain
And squint half-dreaming at the windowpane
Where winter light intensifies to Spring.
I pull the plug so our alarm won't ring.
Then prop myself up on our double bed
And dip to kiss the imprint of your head
And rub your pillow for Aladdin's lamp.
Oh, I'm a sheltered child away in camp!
Get up, she's gone, "Marriage is for the birds."
But who expresses feelings in *those* words?
Stockings, torn underpants litter the floor.
And who's that leering from our bedroom door?
Some empty-head I picked up in a bar.
Those words — she said them last night and, "You're far
Gone hubby. Nurse must bandage baby's heart."
But when she came, I smelled a silent fart.

Tamed by ten years of marriage, I'm polite.
I cook for her so she can have "a bite"
Before she leaves to do her "nine to five"
And "Doesn't screwing make you feel alive?"
I want you now, I don't want a divorce.
Last night I rode a tourist buggy horse
Around the room where Pegasus once flew.
And infidelity? Of course, taboo.
I let her laughing blow my ear, "Goodbye,
You'll still be married on the day you die."

I pace exhausted, though I slept last night.
I watch a jet plane's earnest gray goose flight
Between the roofs: from your apartment here?

I pull a tin ring off a can of beer
And aim the spray against a dirty pane.
Here's to you rain, more promising than rain!
Mark Stern's fizzled out . . . What's chirping? I rub
My finger till the window's clean. A shrub
Downstairs is budding — city warts but green.
Sun smears the ivy with a blinding sheen.
The super cranks her clothesline, conjuring
A flowering branch of colored cotton: Spring!
A bluejay leaves her husband's underwear
To soft-shoe through Manhattan's killing air:
A '20's dandy dressed in top hat, tails.
I rap the window with my fingernails,
But he is "on the town," the stupid thing.
This dying city is no place for Spring.
Or am I just emotionally weak?
I scratch the itchy stubble on my cheek
And dash into the bathroom where I piss
And shave and pick my scalp's psoriasis.
I shout into the mirror football cheers:
You've lived on this stone island thirty years
And loved it for its faults; you are depressed.
Get out, discover it again, get dressed."
        My eye is like a child's; the smog is pot.
Shining cratefuls of plum, peach, apricot
Are flung out of the fruit man's tiny store.
Behind the supermarket glass next door:
Landslides of grapefruit, orange, tangerine,
Persimmon, boysenberry, nectarine.
The florist tilts his giant crayon box
Of yellow roses, daffodils, and phlox.
A Disney sun breaks through, makes toys of trucks
And waddling movers look like Donald Ducks
And joke book captions out of storefront signs:
Cafe du Soir, Austrian Village, Wines.
Pedestrians in olive drabs and grays

Are startled by the sun's kinetic rays,
Then mottled into pointillistic patches.
The light turns green, cars passing hurl out snatches
Of rock-and-roll and Mozart and the weather.
The light turns red. Why aren't we together?

MARK STERN

The guy who's sitting in is not an ass.
My wife and I can only have one child
Because today you can't be middle class
And live in New York City and survive
On less than maybe eighty, ninety grand.
The cost of rent and school here drives me wild.
My daughter wants a sister, brother. I've
Tried to explain to her we can't afford
An extra room, a second bill for school,
That public schools are overcrowded, violent,
That she'd be scared there, or at best be bored.
She looks at me as if I am a fool.
Go make a second-grader understand
I spent ten thousand dollars last year just
For school and camp. The consequence? *I'm* cruel.
Go tell that to the U.S. government
When tax time comes! I work two jobs. My wife
Works one. I know I'm shortening my life
To pay a nanny and a girl to dust.
Crazy. Crazy. Crazy. Why do we stay?
Who would hire a forty-three-year old
Who markets New York City souvenirs?
My wife has tenure at Queens College—gold.
Besides, there is the opera, the ballet,
The theater, restaurants, museums, the stores,
The hi tech energy. Across the street
From us the supermarket stays awake
All night. At 3 A.M. I want some cake,
A hard salami sandwich, eggs and lox?
I put my coat on — and my shoes and socks —

And saunter (unafraid of getting mugged)
To Grand Union or the coffee shop
—The Greek's, who knows I'm sleepless, knows I'm bugged
By money. We commiserate like whores,
Or actors reading that their play's a flop.

When I review the story of my life,
Waiting till thirty-five to have a child,
Till we could learn to live with chronic fear,
Till I could stop bickering with my wife
Because the skimpy future drove us wild . . .
And now she teaches poetry but dreams of money,
And that guy's sitting in to save his soul!
Right on! We're drones and taxes are our honey!
You want to know the hottest souvenir
I sell? A New York City beggar's bowl.
I'm going in to cross my legs and sing
With him, "Oh, we shall overcome someday,"
When rents go down, when they end death and taxes,
When we are not mutated by adapting
— Unable to have the sons we want. I want to say,
The only way it seems you can relax is
To sit in an Eastern position, passive.
These problems both seem petty and feel massive,
And, I'm ashamed to say, just make me numb
To our city's spiritually dying.
I used to call my bourgeois parents "dumb"
And marched, like him, for everybody's rights
But ours. We played at being self-denying
— A comedy— till someone hit the lights!

LIVES OF THE GREAT COMPOSERS

Herr Bruckner often wandered into church
to join the mourners at a funeral.
The relatives of Berlioz were horrified.
"Such harmony," quoth Shakespeare, "is in
immortal souls. . . . We cannot hear it." But
the radio is playing, and outside
rain splashes to the pavement. Now and then
the broadcast fails. On nights like these Schumann
would watch the lightning streak his windowpanes.

Outside the rain is falling on the pavement.
A scrap of paper tumbles down the street.
On rainy evenings Schumann jotted down
his melodies on windowpanes, "Such harmony!
We cannot hear it." The radio goes off and on.
At the rehearsal Gustav Holst exclaimed,
"I'm sick of music, especially my own!"
The relatives of Berlioz were horrified.
Haydn's wife used music to line pastry pans.

On rainy nights the ghost of Mendelssohn
brought melodies for Schumann to compose.
"Such harmony is in immortal souls. . . .
We cannot hear it." One could suppose
Herr Bruckner would have smiled. At Tergensee
the peasants stood to hear young Paganini play,
but here there's lightning, and the thunder rolls.
The radio goes off and on. The rain
falls to the pavement like applause.

A scrap of paper tumbles down the street.
On rainy evenings Schumann would look out
and scribble on the windows of his cell.
"Such harmony." Cars splash out in the rain.
The relatives of Berlioz were horrified
to see the horses break from the cortege
and gallop with his casket to the grave.
Liszt wept to hear young Paganini play.
Haydn's wife used music to line pastry pans.

THE COUNTRY WIFE

She makes her way through the dark trees
Down to the lake to be alone.
Following their voices on the breeze,
She makes her way. Through the dark trees
The distant stars are all she sees.
They cannot light the way she's gone.
She makes her way through the dark trees
Down to the lake to be alone.

The night reflected on the lake,
The fire of stars changed into water.
She cannot see the winds that break
The night reflected on the lake
But knows they motion for her sake.
These are the choices they have brought her:
The night reflected on the lake,
The fire of stars changed into water.

COUNTING THE CHILDREN

I.

"This must have been her bedroom, Mr. Choi.
It's hard to tell. The only other time
I came back here was when I found her body."

Neither of us belonged there. She lived next door.
I was the accountant sent out by the State
To take an inventory of the house.

When someone wealthy dies without a will,
The court sends me to audit the estate.
They know that strangers trust a man who listens.

The neighbor led me down an unlit hall.
We came up to a double door and stopped.
She whispered as if someone else were near.

"She used to wander around town at night
And rifle through the trash. We all knew that.
But what we didn't know about was *them*."

She stepped inside and fumbled for a switch.
It didn't work, but light leaked through the curtains.
"Come in," she said. "I want to show you hell."

I walked into a room of wooden shelves
Stretching from floor to ceiling, wall to wall,
With smaller shelves arranged along the center.

A crowd of faces looked up silently.
Shoulder to shoulder, standing all in rows,
Hundreds of dolls were lining every wall.

Not a collection anyone would want—
Just ordinary dolls salvaged from the trash
With dozens of each kind all set together.

Some battered, others missing arms and legs,
Shelf after shelf of the same dusty stare
As if despair could be assuaged by order.

They looked like sisters huddling in the dark,
Forgotten brides abandoned at the altar,
Their veils turned yellow, dresses stiff and soiled.

Rows of discarded little girls and babies—
Some naked, others dressed for play—they wore
Whatever lives their owners left them in.

Where were the children who promised them love?
The small, caressing hands, the lips which whispered
Secrets in the dark? Once they were woken,

Each by name. Now they have become each other—
Anonymous except for injury,
The beautiful and headless side by side.

Was this where all lost childhoods go? These dim
Abandoned rooms, these crude arrangements staged
For settled dust and shadow, left to prove

That all affection is outgrown, or show
The uniformity of our desire?
How dismal someone else's joy can be.

I stood between the speechless shelves and knew
Dust has a million lives, the heart has one.
I turned away and started my report.

II.

That night I dreamt of working on a ledger,
A book so large it stretched across my desk,
Thousands of numbers running down each page.

I knew I had to settle the account,
Yet as I tried to calculate the total,
The numbers started slipping down the page,

Suddenly breaking up like Scrabble letters
Brushed into a box to end a game,
Each strained-for word uncoupled back to nil.

But as I tried to add them back together
And hold each number on the thin green line
Where it belonged, I realized that now

Nothing I did would ever fit together.
In my hands even $2 + 2 + 2$
No longer equaled anything at all.

And then I saw my father there beside me.
He asked me why I couldn't find the sum.
He held my daughter crying in his arms.

My family stood behind him in a row,
Uncles and aunts, cousins I'd never seen,
My grandparents from China and their parents,

All of my family, living and dead,
A line that stretched as far as I could see
Even the strangers called to me by name.

And now I saw I wasn't at my desk
But working on the coffin of my daughter,
And she would die unless I found the sum.

But I had lost too many of the numbers.
They tumbled to the floor and blazed on fire.
I saw the dolls then—screaming in the flames.

III.

When I awoke, I sat up straight in bed.
The sweaty sheet was twisted in my hands.
My heart was pounding. Had I really screamed?

But no, my wife was still asleep beside me.
I got up quietly and found my robe,
Knowing I couldn't fall asleep again.

Then groping down the unlit hall, I saw
A soft-edged light beneath my daughter's door.
It was the night-light plugged in by her bed.

And I remembered when she was a baby,
How often I would get up in the night
And creep into that room to watch her sleep.

I never told my wife how many times
I came to check each night—or that I was
Always afraid of what I might discover.

I felt so helpless standing by her crib,
Watching the quiet motions of her breath
In the half-darkness of the faint night-light.

How delicate this vessel in our care,
This gentle soul we summoned to the world,
A life we treasured but could not protect.

This was the terror I could not confess—
Not even to my wife—and it was the joy
My daughter had no words to understand.

So standing at my pointless watch each night
In the bare nursery we had improvised,
I learned the loneliness that we call love.

IV.

But I gave up those vigils years ago.
My daughter's seven now, and I don't worry—
At least no more than any father does.

But waking up last night after the dream,
Trembling in the hall, looking at her door,
I let myself be drawn into her room.

She was asleep—the blankets softly rising
And falling with each breath, the faint light tracing
The sleek unfoldings of her long black hair.

Then suddenly I felt my self go numb.
And though you won't believe that an accountant
Can have a vision, I will tell you mine.

Each of us thinks our own child beautiful,
But watching her and marveling at the sheer
Smoothness of skin without a scar or blemish,

I saw beyond my daughter to all children,
And, though elated, still I felt confused
Because I wondered why I never sensed

That thrill of joy when looking at adults
No matter how refined or beautiful,
Why lust or envy always intervened.

There is no *tabula rasa* for the soul.
Each spirit, be it infant, bird or flower,
Comes to the world perfected and complete.

And only time proves its unraveling.
But I'm digressing from my point, my vision.
What I meant to ask is merely this:

What if completion comes only in beginnings?
The naked tree exploding into flower?
And all our prim assumptions about time

Prove wrong? What if we cannot read the future
Because our destiny moves back in time,
And only memory speaks prophetically?

We long for immortality, a soul
To rise up flaming from the body's dust.
I know that it exists. I felt it there,

Perfect and eternal in the way
That only numbers are, intangible but real,
Infinitely divisible yet whole.

But we do not possess it in ourselves.
We die, and it abides, and we are one
With all our ancestors, while it divides

Over and over, common to us all,
The ancient face returning in the child,
The distant arms embracing us, the salt

Of our blind origins filling our veins.
I stood confused beside my daughter's bed
Surprised to find the room around me dim.

Then glancing at the bookshelf in the corner,
I saw she'd lined her dolls up in a row.
Three little girls were sitting in the dark.

Their sharp glass eyes surveyed me with contempt.
They recognized me only as a rival,
The one whose world would keep no place for them.

I felt like holding them tight in my arms,
Promising I would never let them go,
But they would trust no promises of mine.

I feared that if I touched one, it would scream.

GUIDE TO THE OTHER GALLERY

This is the hall of broken limbs
Where splintered marble athletes lie
Beside the arms of cherubim.
Nothing is ever thrown away.

These butterflies are set in rows.
So small and gray inside their case
They look alike now. I suppose
Death makes most creatures commonplace.

These portraits here of the unknown
Are hung three high, frame piled on frame.
Each potent soul who craved renown,
Immortalized without a name.

Here are the shelves of unread books,
Millions of pages turning brown.
Visitors wander through the stacks,
But no one ever takes one down.

I wish I were a better guide.
There's so much more that you should see.
Rows of bottles with nothing inside.
Displays of locks which have no key.

You'd like to go? I wish you could.
This room has such a peaceful view.
Look at that case of antique wood
Without a label. It's for you.

MAZE WITHOUT A MINOTAUR

If we could only push these walls
apart, unfold the room the way
a child might take apart a box
and lay it flat upon the floor—
so many corners cleared at last!
Or else could rip away the roof
and stare down at the dirty rooms,
the hallways turning on themselves,
and understand at last their plan—
dark maze without a minotaur,
no monsters but ourselves.
                              Yet who
could bear to see it all? The slow
descending spirals of the dust
against the spotted windowpane,
the sunlight on the yellow lace,
the hoarded wine turned dark and sour,
the photographs, the letters—all
the crowded closets of the heart.

One wants to turn away—and cry
for fire to break out on the stairs
and raze each suffocating room.
But the walls stay, the roof remains
strong and immovable, and we
can only pray that if these rooms
have memories, they are not ours.

MY CONFESSIONAL SESTINA

Let me confess. I'm sick of these sestinas
written by youngsters in poetry workshops
for the delectation of their fellow students,
and then published in little magazines
that no one reads, not even the contributors
who at least in this omission show some taste.

Is this merely a matter of personal taste?
I don't think so. Most sestinas
are such dull affairs. Just ask the contributors
the last time they finished one outside of a workshop,
even the poignant one on herpes in that new little magazine
edited by their most brilliant fellow student.

Let's be honest. It has become a form for students,
an exercise to build technique rather than taste
and the official entry blank into the little magazines—
because despite its reputation, a passable sestina
isn't very hard to write, even for kids in workshops
who care less about being poets than contributors.

Granted nowadays everyone is a contributor.
My barber is currently a student
in a rigorous correspondence school workshop.
At lesson six he can already taste
success having just placed his own sestina
in a national tonsorial magazine.

Who really cares about most little magazines?
Eventually not even their own contributors

who having published a few preliminary sestinas
send their work East to prove they're no longer students.
They need to be recognized as the new arbiters of taste
so they can teach their own graduate workshops.

Where will it end? This grim cycle of workshops
churning out poems for little magazines
no one honestly finds to their taste?
This ever-lengthening column of contributors
scavenging the land for more students
teaching them to write their boot-camp sestinas?

Perhaps there is an afterlife where all contributors
have two workshops, a tasteful little magazine, and sexy students
who worshipfully memorize their every sestina.

SUMMER STORM

We stood on the rented patio
While the party went on inside.
You knew the groom from college.
I was a friend of the bride.

We hugged the brownstone wall behind us
To keep our dress clothes dry
And watched the sudden summer storm
Floodlit against the sky.

The rain was like a waterfall
Of brilliant beaded light,
Cool and silent as the stars
The storm hid from the night.

To my surprise, you took my arm—
A gesture you didn't explain—
And we spoke in whispers, as if we two
Might imitate the rain.

Then suddenly the storm receded
As swiftly as it came.
The doors behind us opened up.
The hostess called your name.

I watched you merge into the group,
Aloof and yet polite.
We didn't speak another word
Except to say goodnight.

Why does that evening's memory
Return with this night's storm—
A party twenty years ago,
Its disappointments warm?

There are so many *might have beens*,
What ifs that won't stay buried,
Other cities, other jobs,
Strangers we might have married.

And memory insists on pining
For places it never went,
As if life would be happier
Just by being different.

ON THE FERRY, TOWARD PATRAS

Corfu appears, and then the distant blue
draws her away again: uncertain hours
as time begins to drown in voyaging,
no talk, no books, no breakfast taken late.
The sea, divided, falls behind the boat;
I see that blue laid back on darker blue
the way Odysseus must have, when his mind
was emptied of its cleverness at last
by ten years' wandering. His thoughts are mine,
an island without houses, flocks, or trees,
undressed of all its causes. Memory
slides by like waves against the running prow.

What memories could wake my tiredness?
The clothes upon my back, unspoken words
I always carry, wounds from an embrace
too often entered, now are all I own;
along my flesh I feel them hardening,
a frieze that tells the future as the past
and scrolls my progress roundly on my breast.
I cannot keep my secrets to myself.
I am the figure of the ship, and where
I've traveled, where I go, what I will do,
assail and tear aside the simple blue.

REMEMBERING THE ARDÈCHE

April plunges the classroom into light,
aisles of elm trees glitter beyond the window,
and I must pause midsentence, wondering
where you are. En route, no doubt,
chasing the easy skirts of camomile
along the Dordogne, south to Gascony;

while I remain suspended in my lecture,
fistfuls of wit cast before flocks of students
who long for the spring migrations,
chafing at their confinement from the weather.
I wear my patience like a light-green dress
and wear it thin.

It must have been in April
you and I walked together all the way
from Langogne to Aubenas,
never once meeting a window set in a wall
to sever inner from outer; only the high
clearstory of sunny clouds raised upon hills.

THE OLD FISHERMAN

François Dejanna, d. 1980—L'Anse d'Orso, Corsica

He stands beside his ancient, lovely mistress
dreaming of silver fishes caught in the nets,
not of his dozen children, scattered to Calvi,
Ajaccio, who knows where; nor the somber Sunday
visits his wife still pays him, bringing provisions
to go with the bouillabaisse he concocts with lemon
or fennel and (always) a cork. He looks over his lines
woven from rosy silk, like her body at dawn.

Nothing remains this morning of his old passion
but a brace of fishes thrashing on the sand.
The horizon is firmly drawn, like a refusal
to settle with human folly. Cupped in his hand,
she etches its palm with salt, alone among all
the forgotten, whose violence answered to his own.

THE OUTER BANKS

No ornaments but the double bed and open
solitude found in older motels off-season
with solid walls and purely anonymous cells.
Our bed was like a boat drawn up from the gray
Atlantic combing beyond our balcony;
the sound of breakers interwove in the fine
insistent pelt of rain that fell and fell
all weekend while we lingered, beached, protected,
under the sheets folded like canvas sails.

Sometimes we followed the usual path of tourists,
observing drifts of snow and Canada geese
settle into or lift off grassy marshes
through borrowed, diamonded binoculars
that brought them up so close they wavered on
our eye's own rushy edges, made precise
and flat by the forgetting of one dimension.
Flocks in your eye, my love, whole colonies
of gold sparks braving the darkened blue of iris.

We ran with our umbrellas pressed and flattened
like backwards feathers off the pervious wind.
Whenever the sun appeared at intervals
it scared up quarter rainbows in ones and pairs
out of the low bushes like quattrocento
angels. All things brushed across us then:
the braided strands, unbraided, of my hair
glancing your lips and cheek, and of your hands,
the touch that everywhere surprised my own.

BACK TROUBLE

And so to bed. My heart is full of poems,
my pillow full of feathers, unexpressed.
Old traveler, what ails you? Misery,
I've traced so many cities on the ceiling.
I couldn't lift my feet today,
much less my faithful suitcase: Amsterdam,
Florence, and Paris waver on the scrim
superimposed by bad, old-fashioned pain.
One vertebra one centimeter crooked,
and sex and plans and jokes and the blue sky
all vanish in a mist.

                    Where was I? Lost
in the silvery, self-important old wives' tales
that plaster the television, four days deep
in the puzzling, sad, rhetorical *Confessions,*
where stealing a pear is tantamount,
by Augustine's encompassing calculus
of guilt, to shtupping a woman out of bounds,
torturing armies of eremites, or creating
hell as your crater, if you're a fallen angel.
Drink it all down, you pagans, racked in the flesh!
Out of the scarlet bowl. To your health, to mine.

LIFE OF A SALESMAN

Behind the small, fixed windows of the album,
my father sits on sand, flowered with sea-salt,
nestling my younger brothers on his knees,
my mother beside him, me on another towel.

Or else he's smiling, lapped by shallow combers,
holding the kids so only their toes get wet,
free from booze and taxes, the city office,
his territory, miles of empty highway.

My husband, late addition to the family,
points out a disproportion: that generic
photo of my father on the beaches
stands for a man with two weeks' paid vacation.

I say to my brothers, look, you're all contented!
Both of you blue with cold in your ratty towels,
thrilled with the wind, the escalating waves,
our father watching the ocean roll its sevens.

Most of the time, he's on the road again
selling fancy letterhead, engravings
the businessmen he calls on can't be certain
they need, without his powers of persuasion.

He tries to tell them. Fifty weeks a year,
in sun and rain and snow, on secondary
arteries crosshatching the back country
of Pennsylvania, Maryland, West Virginia.

Alone at night in one more shabby diner,
his pale self in the speckled mirror-panels
is like a stranger's. He coats his potatoes
and minute-steak in catsup, for the color.

He wants a drink, but holds off for another
day, another hour. The gray Atlantic
shuffles invisibly. He orders coffee
and maybe calls his sponsor up, long distance.

Or calls my mother next, with lonely questions
she tries to answer, putting on my brothers
who sneeze and whistle, practice words like "daddy"
that touch him at the end of the connection.

The dial tone doesn't sound at all like waves.
He might go to a movie, or a meeting:
there's always one around to fill the shady
dangerous intervals of middle evening.

He likes the coffee's warmth, the sound of voices
circling in on wisdom: know the difference.
Protect him, higher power, when he travels
his hundred miles tomorrow, rain or shine.

His death lies elsewhere, hidden in the future,
far from his wife and children, far away
from cleanly riffled Jersey shores in summer,
the gray Atlantic playing out its hand.

EDEN

In lurid cartoon colors, the big baby
dinosaur steps backwards under the shadow
of an approaching tyrannosaurus rex.
"His mommy going to fix it," you remark,
serenely anxious, hoping for the best.

After the big explosion, after the lights
go down inside the house and up the street,
we rush outdoors to find a squirrel stopped
in straws of half-gnawed cable. I explain,
trying to fit the facts, "The squirrel is dead."

No, you explain it otherwise to me.
"He's sleeping. And his mommy going to come."
Later, when the squirrel has been removed,
"His mommy fix him," you insist, insisting
on the right to know what you believe.

The world is truly full of fabulous
great and curious small inhabitants,
and you're the freshly minted, unashamed
Adam in this garden. You preside,
appreciate, and judge our proper names.

Like God, I brought you here.
Like God, I seem to be omnipotent,
mostly helpful, sometimes angry as hell.
I fix whatever minor faults arise
with bandaids, batteries, masking tape, and pills.

But I am powerless, as you must know,
to chase the serpent sliding in the grass,
or the tall angel with the flaming sword
who scares you when he rises suddenly
behind the gates of sunset.

AMONG PHILISTINES

The night before they meant to pluck his eyes
He caught his tale at six on *Action News*—
Some stylish moron blabbing the bald lies
The public swallowed as "Official Views."

After a word for snuff, Delilah made
A live appearance, and was interviewed.
Complaining what a pittance she was paid,
She plugged the film she starred in in the nude.

Unbearable, he thought, and flipped the switch,
Lay sleepless on the bed in the bright room
Where every thought brought back the pretty bitch
And all the Orient of her perfume,

Her perfect breasts, her hips and slender waist
Matchless among the centerfolds of Zion,
Which summoned to his tongue the mingled taste
Of honey oozing from the rotted lion;

For now his every mumble in the sack
(Bugged, of course, and not a whisper missed)
Would be revealed in lurid paperback
"As told to" Madame Sleaze, the columnist.

Beefcake aside, he was a man of thought
Who heretofore had kept to the strict law:
For all the cheap celebrity it brought
He honestly deplored that ass's jaw,

The glossy covers of their magazines
With taut chains popping on his greasy chest,
The ads for razor blades with the staged scenes
And captions: *Hebrew Hunk Says We Shave Best.*

Such were his thoughts; much more severe the dreams
That sped him through his sleep in a wild car:
Vistas of billboards where he lathered cream,
Gulped milk, chugged beer, or smoked a foul cigar,

And this last image, *this,* mile upon mile:
Delilah, naked, sucking on a pair
Of golden shears, winking her lewdest smile
Amid a monumental pile of hair

And headlines—*Meet the Babe Who Skinned the Yid!*
Starring in just a little offa my head.
He noted how his locks demurely hid
Her tits and snatch. And how her lips were red.

Red as his eyes when he was roused at seven
To trace back to its source the splendid ray
Of sunlight streaming from the throat of Heaven,
Commanding him to kneel and thus to pray:

"Lord God of Hosts, whose name cannot be used
Promotion-wise, whose face shall not adorn
A cornflake box, whose trust I have abused:
Return that strength of which I have been shorn,

That we might smite this tasteless *shiksa* land
With hemorrhoids and rats, with fire and sword.
Forgive my crime. Put forth thy fearsome hand
Against them and their gods, I pray you, Lord. . . ."

So, shorn and strengthless, led through Gaza Mall
Past shoeshop and boutique, Hallmark and Sears,

He held his head erect and smiled to all
And did not dignify the scene with tears,

Knowing that God could mercifully ordain,
For punishment, a blessing in disguise.
"Good riddance," he said, whispering to the pain
As, searing, the twin picks hissed in his eyes.

ANACREONTIC

You drink to piss it all away
You play it tough to seize the day
Toss out more chips and spread your stuff
Or end it with enough's enough
But it doesn't matter what you say
They always seem to call your bluff
It doesn't matter what you do
When you're through you're through

You hit the dirt and slide and slide
Flag down a fox for one last ride
Steal second and go on to third
Or cock the piece and kill the bird
You hope you pray the throw is wide
They'll hold you hold you to your word
And get you down to get you out
When you're out you're out

It's not you didn't do your worst
To quench your everlasting thirst
You kissed them and you made them cry
And didn't wonder how or why
You never even got to first
Toss in the sponge and say good-bye
And let them strip you of the crown
When you're down you're down

It seems a pity seems a crime
They'll get you get you every time
It doesn't matter where you go

Somehow they always seem to know
You're out there but it's closing time
Up to your nuts in drifting snow
Up to your eyes by frosty dawn
When you're gone you're gone

THE DRIVE-IN

Under the neon sign he stands,
My father, tickets in his hands.
Now it is my turn; all the while
Knee-deep in stubs he tries to smile,
Crying, "You'll love it. Slapstick. Fights.
One dollar, please. Please dim your lights."
I pay and enter. Mother waits
In a black truck with dangling plates
And snag-toothed grillwork idling there
On the front row. She combs her hair
And calls for me to take my place.
The moon-lights dying on her face,
She lights another cigarette
And starts to sing the alphabet.
Quickly, I turn the speaker on:
The soundtrack is a steady drone
Of snoring. With his pockets full
My father gathers up his wool,
His pink tongue rolling up and down.
A wolf, dainty in hat and gown,
Appears, sneaking across the screen
Above my father. Then the scene
Expands to show a flock of sheep.
The wolf is drooling; in his sleep
My father smiles, my mother sighs,
And dabbing gently at her eyes
She goes across to sniff his breath.
A shepherd clubs the wolf to death,
The sheep dance lightly in the sun,
And now the feature has begun:

Union Pacific is its name.
I know it, know it frame by frame,
The tyranny of separation,
The lack of all communication
From shore to shore, the struggle through
Smashed chairs and bottles toward the true
Connection of a spike of gold.
I fall asleep. The night is cold.
And waking to the seat's chill touch
I hear the last car's slipping clutch,
As on the glass a veil of frost
Obscures this childhood I have lost.
The show is over. Time descends.
And no one tells me how it ends.

APPROACHING A SIGNIFICANT
BIRTHDAY, HE PERUSES
THE NORTON ANTHOLOGY OF POETRY

All human things are subject to decay.
Beauty is momentary in the mind.
The curfew tolls the knell of parting day.
If Winter comes, can Spring be far behind?

Forlorn! the very word is like a bell
And somewhat of a sad perplexity.
Here, take my picture, though I bid farewell.
In a dark time the eye begins to see.

The woods decay, the woods decay and fall—
Bare ruined choirs where late the sweet birds sang.
What but design of darkness to appall?
An aged man is but a paltry thing.

If I should die, think only this of me:
Crass casualty obstructs the sun and rain
When I have fears that I may cease to be,
To cease upon the midnight with no pain

And hear the spectral singing of the moon
And strictly meditate the thankless muse.
The world is too much with us, late and soon.
It gathers to a greatness, like the ooze.

Do not go gentle into that good night.
Fame is no plant that grows on mortal soil.

Again he raised the jug up to the light:
Old age hath yet his honor and his toil.

Downward to darkness on extended wings,
Break, break, break, on thy cold gray stones, O sea,
And tell sad stories of the death of kings.
I do not think that they will sing to me.

BODY BAGS

I

Let's hear it for Dwayne Coburn, who was small
And mean without a single saving grace
Except for stealing—home from second base
Or out of teammates' lockers, it was all
The same to Dwayne. The Pep Club candy sale,
However, proved his downfall. He was held
Briefly on various charges, then expelled
And given a choice: enlist or go to jail.

He finished basic and came home from Bragg
For Christmas on his reassignment leave
With one prize in his pack he thought unique,
Which went off prematurely New Year's Eve.
The student body got the folded flag
And flew it in his memory for a week.

II

Good pulling guards were scarce in high school ball.
The ones who had the weight were usually slow
As lumber trucks. A scaled-down wild man, though,
Like Dennis "Wampus" Peterson, could haul
His ass around right end for me to slip
Behind his blocks. Played college ball a year—
Red-shirted when they yanked his scholarship
Because he majored, so he claimed, in Beer.

I saw him one last time. He'd added weight
Around the neck, used words like "grunt" and "slope,"
And said he'd swap his Harley and his dope
And both balls for a 4-F knee like mine.
This happened in the spring of '68.
He hanged himself in 1969.

III

Jay Swinney did a great Roy Orbison
Impersonation once at Lyn-Rock Park,
Lip-synching to "It's Over" in his dark
Glasses beside the jukebox. He was one
Who'd want no better for an epitaph
Than he was good with girls and charmed them by
Opening his billfold to a photograph:
Big brother. The Marine. Who didn't die.

He comes to mind, years from that summer night,
In class for no good reason while I talk
About Thoreau's remark that one injustice
Makes prisoners of us all. The piece of chalk
Splinters and flakes in fragments as I write,
To settle in the tray, where all the dust is.

THE CLASSROOM AT THE MALL

Our Dean of Something thought it would be good
For Learning (even better for P.R.)
To make the school 'accessible to all'
And leased the bankrupt bookstore at the Mall
A few steps from Poquito's Mexican Food
And Chocolate Chips Aweigh. So here we are—

Four housewives, several solemn student nurses,
Ms. Light—serious, heavy, and very dark—-
Pete Fontenot, who teaches high-school shop
And is besides a part-time private cop
Who leaves his .38 among the purses,
And I, not quite as thin as Chaucer's Clerk—

Met for our final class while Season's Greetings
Echo subliminally with calls to buy
Whatever this year's ads deem necessary
For Happiness and Joy. The Virgin Mary,
Set up outside to audit our last meetings,
Adores her infant with a glassy eye.

Descend, O Musak! Hail to thee, World Lit!
Hail, Epic ('most of which was wrote in Greek')
And hail three hours deep in Dante's Hell
(The occupants of which no one could spell)—
As much as our tight schedule might admit
Of the Great Thoughts of Man — one thought per week.

I've lectured facing towards 'The Esplanade'
Through plate-glass windows. Ah, what do I see?

Is that the face 'that launched a thousand ships'
Awash with pimples? Oh, those chocolate chips!
Ms. Light breaks in: 'Will this be for a grade?'
It's a good thing the students all face *me*.

One night near Halloween I filled the board
With notes on FAUST. A Pentecostal hair-
Do with a woman underneath looked in,
Copying down my scrawl with a tight grin
That threatened she'd be back with flaming sword
To corner me and Satan in our lair.

Tonight, though, all is calm. They take their quiz
While I sit calculating if I've made
Enough to shop for presents. From my chair
I watch the Christmas window-shoppers stare
At what must seem a novelty, and is,
The Church of Reason in the Stalls of Trade—

Like the blond twins who press against the door,
Accompanied by footsore, pregnant Mummy,
Who tiredly spells out for them the reason
I am not price-tagged as befits the season,
Explaining what is sold in such a store
With nothing but this animated dummy

Who rises, takes the papers one by one
With warm assurances that all shall pass
Because 'requirements have been met,' because
I am an academic Santa Claus,
Because mild-mannered Pete's strapped on his gun.
Ms. Light declares she has enjoyed the class:

'They sure had thoughts, those old guys,' she begins,
Then falters for the rest. And I agree
Because, for once, I've nothing left to say
And couldn't put it better anyway.

I pack the tests, gather my grading pens,
And fumble in my jacket for the key,

With time to spend and promises to keep
And not one 'hidden meaning' to the tale,
Among these drifting schools of moon-eyed teens,
License and credit pulsing in their jeans,
Who circle, hungry for the choice and cheap—
Something of value, soon to go on sale.

RELEASE

Slow for the sake of flowers as they turn
   Toward sunlight, graceful as a line of sail
      Coming into the wind. Slow for the mill—
Wheel's heft and plummet, for the chug and churn
   Of water as it gathers, for the frail
      Half-life of spraylets as they toss and spill.

For all that lags and eases, all that shows
   The winding-downward and diminished scale
      Of days declining to a twilit chill,
Breathe quietly, release into repose:
      Be still.

WAGERS

I bet you don't wear shoulder pads in bed.
I bet when we get over, we'll be *bad!*
I bet you blush all over when you come.

Although the butch coach gave them out, and said,
they're regulation issue for the team,
I bet you don't wear shoulder pads in bed;

and if I whispered something just unseem-
ly enough, I could make your ears turn red.
I bet you blush all over when you come

to where I say, I slept on what we did,
and didn't, then undressed you in a dream.
I bet you don't wear shoulder pads in bed.

I bet my blue pajamas split a seam
while I thought of my hand on you instead.
I bet you blush all over when you come.

Maybe I'll spend Bastille Day feeling bad,
deferring fireworks till the troops get home
—I bet you don't wear shoulder pads in bed.

Don't give me any; just promise me some.
I'm having nicer nightmares than I had.
I bet you blush all over when you come,

but I can bide my time until it's bid-
dable (though, damn, you make me squirm;
I bet you don't wear shoulder pads in bed),

wait till the strawberries are ripe for cream,
and get to give, for having kept my head.
I bet you blush all over when you come.
I bet you don't wear shoulderpads in bed.

"DID YOU LOVE WELL WHAT
VERY SOON YOU LEFT?"

Did you love well what very soon you left?
Come home and take me in your arms and take
away this stomach ache, headache, heartache.
Never so full, I never was bereft
so utterly. The winter evenings drift
dark to the window. Not one word will make
you, where you are, turn in your day, or wake
from your night toward me. The only gift
I got to keep or give is what I've cried,
floodgates let down to mourning for the dead
chances, for the end of being young,
for everyone I loved who really died.
I drank our one year out in brine instead
of honey from the seasons of your tongue.

NIGHTS OF 1964-1966:
THE OLD RELIABLE

For Lewis Ellingham

The laughing soldiers fought to their defeat . . .
James Fenton, "In a Notebook"

White decorators interested in Art,
Black file clerks with theatrical ambitions,
kids making pharamaceutical revisions
in journals Comp. instructors urged they start,
the part-Cherokee teenage genius (maybe),
the secretary who hung out with fairies,
the copywriter wanting to know, where is
my husband? the soprano with the baby,
all drank draft beer or lethal sweet Manhattans
or improvised concoctions with tequila
in summer when, from Third Street, we could feel a
night breeze waft in whose fragrances were Latin.
The place was run by Polish refugees:
squat Margie, gaunt Speedy (whose sobriquet
transliterated what?). He'd brought his play
from Łódź. After a while, we guessed Margie's
illiteracy was why *he* cashed checks
and *she* perched near the threshold to ban pros,
the underage, the fugitive, and those
arrayed impertinently to their sex.
The bar was talk and cruising; in the back
room, we danced: Martha and the Vandellas,
Smokey and the Miracles, while sellers
and buyers changed crisp tens for smoke and smack.
Some came in after work, some after supper,
plumage replenished to meet who knew who.

Behind the bar, Margie dished up beef stew.
On weeknights, you could always find an upper
to speed you to your desk, and drink till four.
Loosened by booze, we drifted, on the ripples
of Motown, home in new couples, or triples,
were back at dusk, with IDs, at the door.
Bill was my roommate, Russell drank with me,
although they were a dozen years my seniors.
I walked off with the eighteen-year-old genius
—an Older Woman, barely twenty-three.
Link was new as Rimbaud, and better looking,
North Beach bar *paideon* of doomed Jack Spicer,
like Russell, our two-meter artificer,
a Corvo whose *ecclesia* was cooking.
Bill and Russell were painters. Bill had been
a monk in Kyoto. Stoned, we sketched together,
till he discovered poppers and black leather
and Zen consented to new discipline.
We shared my Sixth Street flat with a morose
cat, an arch cat, and pot plants we pruned daily.
His boyfriend had left him for an Israeli
dancer; my husband was on Mykonos.
Russell loved Harold, who was Black and bad,
and lavished on him dinners "meant for men"
like Escoffier and Brillat-Savarin.
Staunch blond Dora made rice. When she had
tucked in the twins, six flights of tenement
stairs they'd descend, elevenish, and stroll
down Third Street, desultory night patrol
gone mauve and green under the virulent
streetlights, to the bar, where Bill and I
(if we'd not come to dinner), Link, and Lew,
and Betty had already had a few.
One sweat-soaked night in pitiless July,
wedged on booth benches of cracked Naugahyde,
we planned a literary magazine
where North Beach met the Lower East Side Scene.

We could have titled it *When Worlds Collide*.
Dora was gone, "In case the children wake up."
Link lightly had decamped with someone else
(the German engineer? Or was he Bill's?).
Russell's stooped *vale* brushed my absent makeup.
Armed children spared us home, our good-night hugs
laissez-passer. We railed against the war.
Soon, some of us bused south with SNCC and CORE.
Soon, some of us got busted dealing drugs.
The file clerks took exams and forged ahead.
The decorators' kitchens blazed persimmon.
The secretary started kissing women,
and so did I, and my three friends are dead.

Marilyn Hacker

RUNE OF THE FINLAND WOMAN

For Sára Karig

> "You are so wise," the reindeer said, "you can bind the winds
> of the world in a single strand."
>
> H. C. Anderson, "The Snow Queen"

She could bind the world's winds in a single strand.
She could find the world's words in a singing wind.
She could lend a weird will to a mottled hand.
She could wind a willed word from a muddled mind.

She could wend the wild woods on a saddled hind.
She could sound a wellspring with a rowan wand.
She could bind the wolf's wounds in a swaddling band.
She could bind a banned book in a silken skin.

She could spend a world war on invaded land.
She could pound the dry roots to a kind of bread.
She could feed a road gang on invented food.
She could find the spare parts of the severed dead.

She could find the stone limbs in a waste of sand.
She could stand the pit cold with a withered lung.
She could handle bad puns in the slang she learned.
She could dandle foundlings in their mother tongue.

She could plait a child's hair with a fishbone comb.
She could tend a coal fire in the Arctic wind.
She could mend an engine with a sewing pin.
She could warm the dark feet of a dying man.

She could drink the stone soup from a doubtful well.
She could breathe the green stink of a trench latrine.
She could drink a queen's share of important wine.
She could think a few things she would never tell.

She could learn the hand code of the deaf and blind.
She could earn the iron keys of the frozen queen.
She could wander uphill with a drunken friend.
She could bind the world's winds in a single strand.

ELEVENS

> There is one story and one story only . . .
> Robert Graves, *"To Juan at the Winter Solstice"*

James A. Wright, my difficult older brother,
I'm in an airplane over your Ohio.
Twice a week, there and back, I make this journey
to Cincinnati.

You are six books I own and two I borrowed.
I'm the songs about the drunk on the runway
and leaving your lover for the airport, first
thing in the morning.

You were fifty-two when you died of cancer
of the tongue, apologist for the lonely
girls who were happened to near some bleak water.
Tell me about it.

When my father died young, my mother lost it.
I am only three years younger than he was.
The older brother and the younger brother
that I never had

died young, in foreign cities, uncomforted.
Does anybody not die uncomforted?
My friend Sonny had her lovers around her
and she died also.

Half drunk on sunlight in my second country,
I yearned through six-line stanzas I learned from you.
You spent January of your last winter
upon that mountain.

I love a boy who died and a girl who left.
I love a brother who is a grown woman.
I love your eight books. I hate the ending.
I never knew you.

You knew a lot about airports and rivers
and a girl who went away in October.
Fathers, brothers and sisters die of cancer:
still, we are strangers.

You are the lonely gathering of rivers
below the plane that left you in Ohio;
you are the fog of language on Manhattan
where it's descending.

ELYSIAN FIELDS

"Champs Elysées of Broadway" says the awning
of the café where, every Sunday morning,
young lawyers in old jeans ripped at the knees
do crosswords. Polyglot Lebanese
own it: they've taken on two more shopfronts
and run their banner down all three at once.
Four years ago, their sign, "Au Petit Beurre,"
was so discreet, that, meeting someone there,
I'd tell her the street corner, not the name.
They were in the right place at the right time.
Meanwhile, the poor are trying hard enough.
Outside, on Broadway, people sell their stuff
laid out on blankets, cardboard cartons, towels.
A stout matron with lacquered auburn curls
circles the viridian throw rug
and painted plaster San Martín to hug
a thinner, darker woman, who hugs her
back volubly in Spanish—a neighbor,
I guess, and guess they still have houses.
The man with uncut, browned French paperbacks,
the man with two embroidered gypsy blouses
and three pilled pitiful pairs of plaid slacks
folded beside him on the pavement where
there was a Puerto Rican hardware store
that's been a vacant shopfront for two years
may not. There's a young couple down the block
from our corner; she's tall, gaunt, gangly, Black;
he's short, quick, volatile, unshaven, white.
They set up shop dry mornings around eight.
I've seen him slap her face, jerking her thin

arm like a rag doll's—a dollar kept from him,
she moves too slow, whore, stupid bitch . . . "She's
my wife," he tells a passing man who stops
and watches. If anyone did call the cops
it would be to prevent them and their stacks
of old *Vogues* and outdated science texts
from blocking access to the "upscale bar'"
where college boys get bellicose on beer.
"Leave him," would I say? Does she have keys
to an apartment, to a room, a door
to close behind her? What we meant by "poor"
when I was twenty, was a tenement
with clanking pipes and roaches; what we meant
was up six flights of grimed, piss-pungent stairs,
four babies and a baby-faced welfare
worker forbidden to say "birth control."
I was almost her, on the payroll
of New York State Employment Services
—the East 14th Street Branch, whose task it was
to send day workers, mostly Black, to clean
other people's houses. Five-fifteen
and I walked east, walked south, walked up my four
flights. Poor was a neighbor, was next door,
is still a door away. The door is mine.
Outside, the poor work Broadway in the rain.
The cappuccino drinkers watch them pass
under the awning from behind the glass.

CANCER WINTER

for Rafael Campo and Hayden Carruth

Syllables shaped around the darkening day's
contours. Next to armchairs, on desks, lamps
were switched on. Tires hissed softly on the damp
tar. In my room, a flute concerto played.
Slate roofs glistened in the rain's thin glaze.
I peered out from a cave like a warm bear.
Halls lights flicked on as someone climbed the stairs
across the street, blinked out: a key, a phrase
turned in a lock, and something flew open.
I watched a young man at his window write
at a plank table, one pooled halogen
light on his book, dim shelves behind him, night
falling fraternal on the flux between
the odd and even numbers of the street.

I woke up, and the surgeon said, "You're cured."
Strapped to the gurney, in the cotton gown
and pants I was wearing when they slid me down
onto the table, made new straps secure
while I stared at the hydra-headed O.R.
lamp, I took in the tall, confident, brown-
skinned man, and the ache I couldn't quite call pain
from where my right breast wasn't anymore
to my armpit. A not-yet-talking head,
I bit dry lips. What else could he have said?
And then my love was there in a hospital coat;
then my old love, still young and very scared.
Then I, alone, graphed clock hands' asymptote
to noon, when I would be wheeled back upstairs.

The odd and even numbers of the street
I live on are four thousand miles away
from an Ohio February day
snow-blanketed, roads iced over, with sleet
expected later, where I'm incomplete
as my abbreviated chest. I weigh
less—one breast less—since the Paris-gray
December evening, when a neighbor's feet
coming up ancient stairs, the feet I counted
on paper were the company I craved.
My calm right breast seethed with a grasping tumor.
The certainty of my returns amounted
to nothing. After terror, being brave
became another form of gallows humor.

At noon, an orderly wheeled me upstairs
via an elevator hung with Season's
Greetings streamers, bright and false as treason.
The single room the surgeon let us share
the night before the knife was scrubbed and bare
except for blush-pink roses in a vase on
the dresser. Veering through a morphine haze on
the cranked bed, I was avidly aware
of my own breathing, my thirst, that it was over—
the week that ended on this New Year's Eve.
A known hand held, while I sipped, icewater,
afloat between ache, sleep, lover and lover.
The one who stayed would stay; the one would leave.
The hand that held the cup next was my daughter's.

It's become a form of gallows humor
to reread the elegies I wrote
at that pine table, with their undernote
of cancer as death's leitmotiv, enumer-
ating my dead, the unknown dead, the rumor
of random and pandemic deaths. I thought
I was a witness, a survivor, caught

in a maelstrom and brought forth, who knew more
of pain than some, but learned it loving others.
I need to find another metaphor
while I eat up stories of people's mothers
who had mastectomies. "She's eighty-four
this year, and *fine!*" Cell-shocked, I brace to do
what I can, an unimportant exiled Jew.

The hand that held the cup next was my daughter's
—who would be holding shirts for me to wear,
sleeve out, for my bum arm. She'd wash my hair
(not falling yet), strew teenager's disorder
in the kitchen, help me out of the bathwater.
A dozen times, she looked at the long scar
studded with staples, where I'd suckled her,
and didn't turn. She took me / I brought her
to the surgeon's office, where she'd hold
my hand, while his sure hand, with its neat tool, snipped
the steel, as on a revised manuscript
radically rewritten since my star
turn nursing her without a "nursing bra"
from small, firm breasts, a twenty-five-year-old's.

I'm still alive, an unimportant Jew
who lives in exile,voluntarily
or not: Ohio's alien to me.
Death follows me home here, but I pay dues
to stay alive. White cell count under two:
a week's delay in chemotherapy
stretches it out: Ohio till July?
The Nazarenes and Pentecostals who
think drinking wine's a mortal sin would pray
for me to heal, find Jesus, go straight, leave.
But I'm alive, and can believe I'll stay
alive a while. Insomniac with terror,
I tell myself, it isn't the worst horror.
It's not Auschwitz. It's not the Vel d'Hiv.

I had "breasts like a twenty-five-year-old,"
and that was why, although a mammogram
was done the day of my year-end exam
in which the doctor found the lump, it told
her nothing: small, firm, dense breasts have and hold
their dirty secrets till their secrets damn
them. Out of the operating room
the tumor was delivered, sectioned, cold-
packed, pickled, to demonstrate to residents
an infiltrative ductal carcinoma
(with others of its kind). I've one small, dense
firm breast left, and cell-killer pills so no more
killer cells grow, no eggs drop. To survive
my body stops dreaming it's twenty-five.

It's not Auschwitz. It's not the Vel d'Hiv.
It's not gang rape in Bosnia or
gang rape and gutting in El Salvador.
My self-betraying body needs to grieve
at how hatreds metastasize. Reprieved
(if I am), what am I living for?
Cancer, gratuitous as a massacre,
answers to nothing, tempts me to retrieve
the white-eyed panic in the mortal night,
my father's silent death at forty-eight,
each numbered, shaved, emaciated Jew
I might have been. They wore the blunt tattoo,
a scar, if they survived, oceans away.
Should I tattoo my scar? What would it say?

No body stops dreaming it's twenty-five,
or twelve, or ten, when what is possible's
a long road poplars curtain against loss, able
to swim the river, hike the culvert, drive
through the open portal, find the gold hive
dripping with liquid sweetness. Risible
fantasy, if, all the while, invisible

entropies block the roads, so you arrive
outside a ruin, where trees bald with blight
wane by a river drained to sluggish mud.
The setting sun looks terribly like blood.
The hovering swarm has nothing to forgive.
Your voice petitions the indifferent night:
"I don't know how to die yet. Let me live."

Should I tattoo my scar? What would it say?
It could say "K.J.'s Truck Stop" in plain Eng-
lish, highlighted with a nipple ring
(the French version: Chez K.J. / Les Routiers).
I won't be wearing falsies, and one day
I'll bake my chest again at Juan-les-Pins,
round side and flat, gynandre/androgyne,
close by my love's warm flanks (though she's sun-shy
as I should be: it's a carcinogen
like smoked fish, caffeine, butterfat and wine).
O let me have my life and live it too!
She kissed my breasts, and now one breast she kissed
is dead meat, with its pickled blight on view.
She'll kiss the scar, and then the living breast.

I don't know how to die yet. Let me live!
Did Etty Hillesum think that, or Anne Frank,
or the forty-year-old schoolteacher the bank
robber took hostage when the cop guns swiv-
eled on them both, or the seropositive
nurse's aide, who, one long-gone payday, drank
too much, fucked whom? or the bag lady who stank
more than I wished as I came closer to give
my meager change? I say it, bargaining
with the *contras* in my blood, immune
system bombarded but on guard. Who's gone?
The bookseller who died at thirty-nine,
poet, at fifty-eight, friend, fifty-one,
friend, fifty-five. These numbers do not sing.

She'll kiss the scar, and then the living breast,
and then, again, from ribs to pit, the scar,
but only after I've flown back to her
out of the unforgiving Middle West
where my life's strange, and flat disinterest
greets strangers. At Les-Saintes-Maries-de-la-Mer,
lust pulsed between us, pulsed in the plum grove where
figs dropped to us like manna to the blessed.
O blight that ate my breast like worms in fruit,
be banished by the daily pesticide
that I ingest. Let me live to praise
her breathing body in my arms, our wide-
branched perennial love, from whose taproot
syllables shape around the lengthening days.

Friends, you died young. These numbers do not sing
your requiems, your elegies, our war
cry: at last, not "Why me?" but "No more
one-in-nine, one-in-three, rogue cells killing
women." You're my companions, traveling
from work to home to the home I left for
work, and the plague, and the poison which might cure.
The late sunlight, the morning rain, will bring
me back to where I started, whole, alone,
with fragrant coffee into which I've poured
steamed milk, book open on the scarred pine table.
I almost forget how close to the bone
my chest's right side is. Unremarkable,
I woke up, still alive. Does that mean "cured"?

JOURNEY OUT

Say that you're lying comfortably under
the weather. Outside world? A passer-by
whose shadow barely skims the lukewarm puddle
of reverie you drown in as you lie.

Bruised but not feverish, you stretch and drowse,
minimally drugged against the pain.
An opalescent country's taking shape:
carpet, oasis, palms, a golden plain.

Pursed lips are blowing up a green balloon.
Spring; birthday party; training bra; the park.
Now gasp for air before the flashbulbs pop
their cameos and leave you in the dark.

Each dear desire is equidistant. Shut
your eyes and let a pin-pricked map direct
your journey. The arrival is what's hard.
Take off that aching carcass and climb out.

On nameless pebbles the ship grinds to a halt.
Gaggles of children are whisked out of sight
by mothers who replace them at the windows
(masked by lace curtains) in the looming night.

Only a single tavern is lit up.
With the swart owner and his pasty wife
you sit by a green wall and drink a toast
to this unheard-of life.

SENTIMENTAL EDUCATION

When my eyes rove in search of recognition,
what fills them, as if they were ears, not eyes,
is nothing I can see, but roaring surf,
its nightly entertainment and announcement
when I lived on the island. All night long
it used to grind an endless message out
and never climb the beach. I used to gaze
blankly as if by staring I could scan
in that white band of sound some rune of future
and not of future only. Present too.
As if by paying close enough attention
I could decipher the illegible
story of my life and what it stood for;
a glass partition only broached in dreams
again erected with each day, again
and always an enigma. And if I
couldn't read the riddle, then who could?
I listened to the waves as if they led
to further signs, to ramifying maps
of passage in a life for me to choose.
Once I knelt down between a rusty tractor
and a puddle of orange water dwindling
on cracked cement under the noon sun
and tried to pray. And once
I heard a kitten's or an infant's mewl
leak from between my twenty-five year-old lips.
There was no other sound,
there was no father left, I had to mother
myself, there were in fact
no instructions past my own nose.

Oh yes, the flaming sunsets; yes, the surf's
portentous growling. But the sea was mute,
the rosy dawns were dumb, the granite mountain.
Turning my back on these would tell no secrets;
but even zero veiled itself from me
until I tore myself away like skin
and walked into the story of the future.

MOMENTS OF SUMMER

i

Let gleaming motes of hayseed in the barn
be asterisks embedded in the text
of ever after. Over by the lawn
let the hammock be an ampersand
skewed to the horizontal, loosely slung
between an evergreen and larch whose sap
sometimes bedews the dreamer in suspension.
Let the book left open on her lap
and on whose margins scattered symbols mark
tempo as slow, as slower, as quite still,
guide her between this twilight and the next.
The swinging stops. Behind the pine-treed hill
Venus appears to herald in the green
slumber of gardens growing in the dark.

ii

June's supple weavings covered up the dry
tank winter had just drained. So did it fill?
Not yet. The least green gesture halted me.
A sundial blandly bedded among flowers
foreshadows a beginning or an end,
silently tells the passing of the hours:
that promise, that futility, that beauty.
Each summer points to picnics on the hill.
What if what falters is the sheer desire
to scale even our modest little mound,

look over treetops, steeples, see the whole?
Somewhere invisible a chainsaw roars.
Precisely where pines creak and sway and fall
is muffled in imagination's veil.

iii

The horizontal tugs me more and more.
Childhood hours spent reading with my father
rise in a kind procession once again.
Disparate gravities of our two ages
dissolve as we lie back and let the pages
take us, float us, sail us out to sea.
What special spell (not always narrative;
the winter we read "De Senectute"
I was fifteen; you had two years to live)
braided our endless differences to one?
Today a mother reading to my son,
I savor freshly that sweet nourishment,
timeless hours reading motionless together,
especially if we are lying down.

THREE SILENCES

I

Of all the times when not to speak is best,
mother's and infant's is the easiest,
the milky mouth still warm against her breast.

Before a single year has passed, he's well
along the way: language has cast its spell.
Each thing he sees now has a tale to tell.

A wide expanse of water: ocean. Look!
Next time, it seems that water is a brook.
The world's loose leaves, bound up into a book.

II

The habit holds for love. He wants to seize
lungsful of ardent new sublimities.
Years gradually pry him loose from these.

He comes to prize a glance's eloquence,
learning to construct a whole romance
from hint and gesture, meaning carved from chance.

And finally silence. Nothing in a phrase
so speaks of love as an averted gaze,
sonnets succumbing to remembrances.

III

At the Kiwanis traveling carnival
I ride beside you on the carousel.
You hold on solemnly, a little pale.

I don't stretch out my hand. You ride alone.
Each mother's glance reduplicates my own;
the baffled arc, the vulnerable bone.

Myself revolving in the mirror's eye
as we go round beneath a cloudy sky,
eyeing my little boy attentively,

I swallow what I was about to say
(no loving admonition is the way
to bridge this gap) and hear the music play

and later, wordless, reach and lift you down
over the rigid horse's shiny brown
mane, and press your body close against my own.

Stillness after motion,
the creaky music cranking, cranking down,
the carnival preparing to leave town.

THE RED HAT

It started before Christmas. Now our son
officially walks to school alone.
Semi-alone, it's accurate to say:
I or his father track him on the way.
He walks up on the east side of West End,
we on the west side. Glances can extend
(and do) across the street; not eye contact.
Already ties are feeling and not fact.
Straus Park is where these parallel paths part;
he goes alone from there. The watcher's heart
stretches, elastic in its love and fear,
toward him as we see him disappear,
striding briskly. Where two weeks ago,
holding a hand, he'd dawdle, dreamy, slow,
he now is hustled forward by the pull
of something far more powerful than school.

The mornings we turn back to are no more
than forty minutes longer than before,
but they feel vastly different—flimsy, strange,
wavering in the eddies of this change,
empty, unanchored, perilously light
since the red hat vanished from our sight.

SAINTS AND STRANGERS

1. *At the Piano*

One night two hunters, drunk, came in the tent.
They fired their guns and stood there stupidly
as Daddy left the pulpit, stalked toward them,
and slapped them each across the mouth. He split
one's upper lip.
              They beat him like a dog.
They propped their guns against the center pole,
rolled up their sleeves as Daddy stood and preached
about the desecration of God's house.
They punched him down, took turns kicking his ribs,
while thirty old women and sixteen men
sat slack-jawed in their folding chairs and watched.
Just twelve, not knowing what to do, I launched
into "Amazing Grace"—the only hymn
I knew by heart—and everybody sang.
We sang until the hunters grew ashamed
—or maybe tired—and left, taking their guns,
their faces red and gleaming from the work.

They got three years suspended sentence each
and Daddy got another tale of how
Christians are saints and strangers in the world.
I guess he knows. He said that I'd done right
to play the song. God's music saved his life.
But I don't know. I couldn't make a guess.
Can you imagine what it means to be
just barely twelve, a Christian and a girl,
and see your father beaten to a pulp?

Neither can I, God knows, and I was there
in the hot tent, beneath the mildewed cloth,
breathing the August, Alabama air,
and I don't know what happened there, to me.
I told this to my second husband, Jim.
We were just dating then. I cried a lot.
He said, *Hush, dear, at least your father got*
a chance to turn all four of his cheeks.
I laughed. I knew, right then, I was in love.
But still I see that image of my father,
his weight humped on his shoulders as he tried
to stand, and I kept plunging through the song
so I could watch my hands and not his face,
which was rouged crimson with red clay and blood.

2. Eve's Sin

Some summer nights when we were on the road
we slept in sleeping bags inside the tent—
money. I'd listen to mosquitoes sing,
how they go oddly silent as they strike.
If I were bored enough I'd let them land
and fill themselves with blood. Then I'd decide
if I would let them go or slap them dead,
knowing I'd wake to find the purple flecks
smudged randomly across my neck and arms.

As I removed my dress to go to sleep,
I saw my underpants were dark with blood.
There wasn't any pain but I was scared.
I called, *Daddy?* He said, *Hush, Marie.*
I said, *I'm bleeding, Daddy.* He was strange,
yet happy too. He held my hands and said,
This happens to all little girls. I should
have mentioned it. You'll bleed like this each month—
about five days. It's . . . He paused and thought,

and that long pause scared me so bad I cried
until I vomited. It sounded so
illogical. I was convinced that I
was dying. It took me years to figure out
that he'd almost explained the sin of Eve
which every woman suffers for. But that
was years later. He rocked me like a child.
He whispered, *Hush now, Baby. Hush yourself,*
kissed my drenched cheeks, and zipped me in the bag,
an undershirt clenched hard between my thighs.

3. *Where the River Jordan Ends*

She put two flowered hair clasps in my hair.
They held. I was amazed. Though Daddy thought
I should be wearing ribbons on my head
he couldn't make them stay. One Christmas Day
he saved the ribbons left from opening gifts
and looped them through my curls. We went to church,
where Aunt Bess snickered, picked them from my hair
and off my neck. She told Daddy, *Jerome,*
she's festooned like a nigger Christmas tree.
But Mrs. Shores knew everything! She smiled
and smoothed my hair around the flowered clasps.
Her husband had invited Daddy down
to preach a week's revival at his church,
and she, since I was almost thirteen, let me
drink coffee when the men were off at work.

Their son took me and Sis into the church.
We ran around the aisles till we got tired,
then shucked our shoes and socks, sat on the rail,
and dangled feet into the River Jordan—
a painting on the wall that seemed to flow
into the baptistery. We splashed around,
got wet, then stripped down to our birthday suits,

and leapt into the font. We went berserk.
We were cannonballing off the rail
when Daddy threw the double doors apart.
We jumped into the font and held our breaths.
When I came up, Daddy was standing there,
waiting. I flinched. Instead he touched my cheek:
Put on your clothes, Elizabeth Marie.
And then I saw the tears. I cried all day.
That night as I sat staring at the wall
behind my father, where the Jordan ends,
I heard God's voice and went to be immersed,
trembling and happy in a paper robe,
and Daddy hugged my body to his chest.
I left a wet, dark shadow on his suit.
I wanted to be saved again. Again.

4. Loose Change

We'd sip our water and wait till supper came,
then he'd return thanks. It was never quick
or done by rote. It was heartfelt—and loud—
while everybody in the truck stop watched.
They tried to do it secretly, the way
you look at cripples, retards, droolers, freaks.
I'd raise my head and watch them watching us,
and once, seeing my head unbowed, he said,
Elizabeth Marie, please close your eyes.
He says that we are strangers here on earth
and it is true I've never felt at home.
In Denver, once, a man asked me the way
to Mile High Stadium, and though I'd been
in town almost two years and had a job
I said, *I'm a stranger here myself,*
amazed at what was coming from my lips.
Are you okay? he asked. How could I say
that I'd been talking bad theology?

But it was worse for Daddy, I suspect.
At least I watched the world and tried to make
accommodation. Since he wouldn't tip
I lifted loose change from the offering plate
to slip onto the table as we left.
Staring right at the waitress, I would think,
Take this, you slut, I've stolen it for you.

5. The Southern Crescent Was On Time

I played piano while my daddy knelt,
unlaced their shoes, and washed the clean pink feet
they'd washed before they'd come to have them washed.
He never just slopped water on the feet
like some men do. Instead he'd lift each foot,
working the soapy rag between their toes
with such relentless tenderness the boys
would giggle, girls would blush, and women sigh.
And though the feet looked clean to begin with,
when he was done the water was as black
as crankcase oil.
                          And then he'd preach, preach hard.
Black suit, black tie, white shirt gone limp with heat,
he'd slap the pulpit and a spray of sweat
would fly into the air. He'd wipe his brow,
letting the silence work into the crowd,
and then start low, or with—almost—a shout.
I never could guess which. His face would gleam
with sweat. It was as if he were, each night,
baptizing himself from the inside out.

As you drive home tonight, he'd say, *a truck
a diesel truck,*
                          might cross into your lane
and you would die apart from God,
                                                  unsaved.
One night a pair of twins sat in this tent

and each one heard God speaking to his heart.
One twin came forward to be saved,

       and one

stayed in his seat,

     resisted God's free grace.
He needed time to think—or so he thought—
but you can't know when God will take you back.
The earth is not our home. We're passing through.
That night

    as they drove to the Dairy Queen
their brand-new car stalled on the railroad track.
That night

    the Southern Crescent was on time.
One went to heaven with his loving God,
and we know where the other went,

      don't we?
The place where you are bathed in clinging fire
and it will last forever,

    burning, burning,
and you will beg to die.

    But you can't die
because, poor fool,

   you are already dead.

He'd wipe his forehead with a handkerchief.

If you should die tonight where will your soul
reside for all eternity?

    In fire?
Or will you sit, in grace, at God's right hand?
Come up for God's free cleansing love.

      Come up.

Let Jesus take your sins away.

    Come up.

They'd come and Daddy would dunk them on the spot
so they could face the family car in peace.
Waiting for them as they lurched down the aisle,

he stood, head bowed, arms raised above his head,
and I would play until his hands came down
and touched his belt. And once I played
twenty-two verses of "Just As I Am"
while Daddy stood there stubbornly, arms raised,
waiting for God to move their hardened hearts.
I prayed that someone would be saved. My sweat
dripped on my hands. My fingers cramped
and skittered on the keys, then I passed out.

When I came to,
the crowd was gone and Daddy's coat was tucked
beneath my head. He rubbed my arms, rolling
the limp flesh back and forth between his hands.
His eyes were focused past the empty chairs
and out the door. His lips moved silently
so I could tell he was praying for me.
But what, I didn't ask or want to know.

6. *A Kiss in Church*

I had to giggle at the way he sang
"Amazing Grace" like Donald Duck. And once,
while everybody's head was bowed, he kissed
me on the mouth. But Daddy saw the kiss
and later, after church, he yelled at me.
I was too big—too old—for him to slap.
He wouldn't stop yelling. I wouldn't cry
or say that I'd done wrong. Next thing I knew
I was married. Though Daddy says I was,
I don't remember being asked. Bud was
a handsome boy. So Daddy could be right.
But for the longest time after I left
I kept this scene to jab into my heart:
Bud sitting, dirty, at the kitchen table,
his flannel sleeves rolled past his elbows.

He's giving me that hangdog look of his
as I stand in the doorway, adamant,
my second baby straddling my hip.
How can he be so meaningless, who once
was everything? And what am I to him?
Nothing. I hope nothing. Nothing at all.

7. *Glossolalia*

There was one sagging bed, all his. We slept
on quilts—a pallet in the living room—
and listened to his shallow, rasping breaths
assert themselves against the growl and suck
of diesels on the interstate. They made
the whole house shake. While Sis was off at work
I wiped dried Maalox from his lips, fed him,
and prayed as best I could. And I'd call home
and talk for hours to the girls and Jim
until I couldn't tell the phone calls from
the prayers. Daddy's speech returned to English
and we could understand, at last, the words,
which up till then had been a random, wild
intensity of esses. It sounded like
the tongues of fire, the glossolalia
that slithers off the otherworldly tongues
of people baptized in the Holy Ghost.
His demons suddenly were visible
and he'd been talking to them in a tongue
we couldn't understand. It frightened us.
It was like we were children once again
and there was Daddy once again endowed
with knowledge of a world we couldn't see.

When he walked off, the sheriff brought him back
and helped me tuck him in. Over iced tea,
he said that Daddy'd run through Kroger's, shouting,

and pointing out the demons. One lady screamed
when Daddy shouted in her face, *My God!*
One's chewing on your ear! The sheriff thought
that was a hoot. He laughed and slapped his thigh.
At supper Sis got mad and screamed at me
for letting him stray off. I let it slide
and passed the meat. That night, rising to pee,
I found her curled up on Daddy's bed.
He was asleep and she was sleeping too,
her face unaging as she shed the world,
and she was shining: light trickled down her face,
her cheeks. It shone like streams of molten solder.
Silver would sound more beautiful and it
was beautiful. It took my breath away.
But I have never seen molten silver.
Or molten glass.
                I made my mind up then
she didn't have the strength to care for Daddy.
It was my turn. Before I left, we sold
the loaded truck, the folding chairs, the tent.
Almost nine hundred bucks. The root of evil.
Enough for her to let her sainthood go.
And if I wouldn't change a thing—not this,
not anything—is that a lack of faith?
Too much imagination? Not enough?

8. *Saints and Strangers*

You teach a Baptist etiquette, she turns
Episcopalian. I did. It's calm.
And Daddy, who shudders when I take the host,
stays home and worships with the TV set.
He's scared to leave the house. Incontinence.
When he's wet himself, he lets us know
by standing grimly at our bedroom door
and reading from his Bible. We think about

a nursing home. If I put on Ray Charles
he huffs around the house and says, *Marie,*
that nigger jungle-thumping hurts my head.
But these are little things. In many ways
the stroke has helped. He's gentle with the girls.
For hours he'll ride them horsy on his knees.
Still, there are those damn demons. Mine are blue,
Jim's red. He whispers demons to the girls
and gets them so they don't know what to think
of us. Beth's asthma starts. I tell the girls,
You play pretend, don't you? Well, you can stop.
But Paw-paw can't. He always plays pretend.
They seem to understand. In some ways, though,
I think he's even purer now—a saint
of all his biases, almost beyond
the brute correction of our daily lives.
Strangeness is part of it. And rage and will.
There's something noble in that suffering
and something stupid too. I'm not a saint,
of course, but as a child I had a rage
I've lost to age, to sex, to understanding,
which takes the edge off everything. Perhaps
it's my metabolism cooling down.
Who knows? One glory of a family is
you'd never choose your kin and can't unchoose
your daddy's hazel eyes—no more than you
could unchoose your hand. You get to be,
in turn, someone you'd never choose to be.
When feeling strong, I'll ask him to give thanks.
If he goes on too long, I say amen
and pass whatever bowl is near at hand.
Jim carves the meat, the girls reach for their tea,
and Daddy takes the bowl and helps his plate.

THE HEREAFTER

Some people as they die grow fierce, afraid.
They see a bright light, offer frantic prayers,
and try to climb them, like Jacob's ladder, up
to heaven. Others, never wavering,
inhabit heaven years before they die,
so certain of their grace they can describe,
down to the gingerbread around the eaves,
the cottage God has saved for them. For hours
they'll talk of how the willow will not weep,
the flowering Judas not betray. They'll talk
of how they'll finally learn to play the flute
and speak good French.
                                    Still others know they'll rot
and their flesh turn to earth, which will become
live oaks, spreading their leaves in August light.
The green cathedral glow that shines through them
will light grandchildren playing hide-and-seek
inside the grove. My next-door neighbor says
he's glad the buzzards will at last give wings
to those of us who've envied swifts as they
swoop, twist, and race through tight mosquito runs.

And some—my brother's one—anticipate
the grave as if it were a chair pulled up
before a fire on winter nights. His ghost,
he thinks, will slouch into the velvet cushion,
a bourbon and branchwater in its hand.
I've even met a man who says the soul
will come back in another skin—the way
a renter moves from house to house. Myself,

I'd like to come back as my father's hound.
Or something fast: a deer, a rust-red fox.

For so long I have thought of us as nails
God drives into the oak floor of this world,
it's hard to comprehend the hammer turned
to claw me out. I'm joking, mostly. I love
the possibilities—not one or two
but all of them. So if I had to choose,
pick only one and let the others go,
my death would be less strange, less rich, less like
a dizzying swig of fine rotgut. I roll
the busthead, slow, across my tongue and taste
the copper coils, the mockingbird that died
from fumes and plunged, wings spread, into the mash.
And underneath it all, just barely there,
I find the scorched-nut hint of corn that grew
in fields I walked, flourished beneath a sun
that warmed my skin, swaying in a changing wind
that tousled, stung, caressed, and toppled me.

Andrew Hudgins

DEAD CHRIST

There seems no reason he should've died. His hands
are pierced by holes too tidy to have held,
untorn, hard muscles as they writhed on spikes.
And on the pink, scrubbed bottom of each foot
a bee-stung lip pouts daintily.
No reason he should die—and yet, and yet
Christ's eyes are swollen with it, his mouth
hangs slack with it, his belly taut with it,
his long hair lank with it, and damp;
and underneath the clinging funeral cloth
his manhood's huge and useless with it: Death.

One blood-drop trickles toward his wrist. Somehow
the grieving women missed it when they bathed,
today, the empty corpse. Most Christs return.
But this one's flesh. He isn't coming back.

PRAYING DRUNK

Our Father who art in heaven, I am drunk.
Again. Red wine. For which I offer thanks.
I ought to start with praise, but praise
comes hard to me. I stutter. Did I tell you
about the woman whom I taught, in bed,
this prayer? It starts with praise; the simple form
keeps things in order. I hear from her sometimes.
Do you? And after love, when I was hungry,
I said, *Make me something to eat.* She yelled,
Poof! You're a casserole!—and laughed so hard
she fell out of bed. Take care of her.

Next, confession—the dreary part. At night
deer drift from the dark woods and eat my garden.
They're like enormous rats on stilts except,
of course, they're beautiful. But why? What *makes*
them beautiful? I haven't shot one yet.
I might. When I was twelve, I'd ride my bike
out to the dump and shoot the rats. It's hard
to kill your rats, our Father. You have to use
a hollow point and hit them solidly.
A leg is not enough. The rat won't pause.
Yeep! Yeep! it screams, and scrabbles, three-legged, back
into the trash, and I would feel a little bad
to kill something that wants to live
more savagely than I do, even if
it's just a rat. My garden's vanishing.
Perhaps I'll merely plant more beans, though that
might mean more beautiful and hungry deer.
Who knows?

I'm sorry for the times I've driven
home past a black, enormous, twilight ridge.
Crested with mist, it looked like a giant wave
about to break and sweep across the valley,
and in my loneliness and fear I've thought,
O let it come and wash the whole world clean.
Forgive me. This is my favorite sin: despair—
whose love I celebrate with wine and prayer.

Our Father, thank you for all the birds and trees,
that nature stuff. I'm grateful for good health,
food, air, some laughs, and all the other things
I'm grateful that I've never had to do
without. I have confused myself. I'm glad
there's not a rattrap large enough for deer.
While at a zoo last week, I sat and wept
when I saw one elephant insert his trunk
into another's ass, pull out a lump,
and whip it back and forth impatiently
to free the goodies hidden in the lump.
I could have let it mean most anything,
but I was stunned again at just how little
we ask for in our lives. *Don't look! Don't look!*
Two young nuns tried to herd their giggling
schoolkids away. *Line up,* they called. *Let's go
and watch the monkeys in the monkey house.*
I laughed, and got a dirty look. Dear Lord,
we lurch from metaphor to metaphor,
which is—let it be so—a form of praying.

I'm usually asleep by now—the time
for supplication. Requests. As if I'd stayed
up late and called the radio and asked
they play a sentimental song. Embarrassed.
I want a lot of money and a woman.
And, also, I want vanishing cream. You know—
a character like Popeye rubs it on

and disappears. Although you see right through him,
he's there. He chuckles, stumbles into things,
and smoke that's clearly visible escapes
from his invisible pipe. It makes me think,
sometimes, of you. What makes me think of me
is the poor jerk who wanders out on air
and then looks down. Below his feet, he sees
eternity, and suddenly his shoes
no longer work on nothingness, and down
he goes. As I fall past, remember me.

TWO EMBER DAYS IN ALABAMA

I.

Out with my dog at dawn—we couldn't sleep—
I met a woman hanging laundry, mist
rising from warm, wet clothes. The empty forms
flapped on the line like pieces of three ghosts
filling with wind before they froze. And further on,
in woods, I saw the vaguely hourglass shape
my boot had stamped in mud the day before,
and, frozen in it, the hoofprint of a deer.
Dan sniffed it, whined, jerked at the leash, his nose
aimed low into the brambled underbrush.
We circled home past bright clothes frozen stiff.
Like pendulums, they ticktocked in the wind.

I shivered underneath cold, rumpled sheets
and so did Dan, who warmed my feet. At noon
we didn't budge. Rain, like a gray hammer, fell.
But now my footprints and the deer's have merged
in mud, the wild spring loosening of earth.

II.

My tomcats saunter from near woods, and when
I hold them, resisting, up against my cheek
I smell—what is it? Smoke, confused with fur.
And now, in deepest Lent, an Ember day,
I marvel at the inconclusive whiff of fire
that lingers there. This Lent, too, lingers on

like twilight or the study of last things.
The blackbirds peck through dried-up winter weeds.
There's nothing much to eat that I can see,
but they are fat and glossy as eight balls.
As I walk out the door, they rise and join
the northward stream of blackbirds, grackles, crows
that have for days been building energy
for exodus. They've swelled the barren woods,
loading the unleaved trees like the black fruit
of nothingness. And now they simply leave.
First fall, then winter. Then this long pause. And then
the starting over. And then the never-ending.

ELEGY FOR MY FATHER,
WHO IS NOT DEAD

One day I'll lift the telephone
and be told my father's dead. He's ready.
In the sureness of his faith, he talks
about the world beyond this world
as though his reservations have
been made. I think he wants to go,
a little bit—a new desire
to travel building up, an itch
to see fresh worlds. Or older ones.
He thinks that when I follow him
he'll wrap me in his arms and laugh,
the way he did when I arrived
on earth. I do not think he's right.
He's ready. I am not. I can't
just say good-bye as cheerfully
as if he were embarking on a trip
to make my later trip go well.
I see myself on deck, convinced
his ship's gone down, while he's convinced
I'll see him standing on the dock
and waving, shouting, *Welcome back.*

THE TELLING

Dawn overtook Scheherazade and she fell silent.
"Hey, Mister Antisocial, Mister Unconscious—
come join the family," Mom called. Ignored her.
"Nerd, nerd, nerd is the word," my uncle sang.
Fuck him. It's night again. Scheherazade
tells of the fisherman who caught four fish:
one red, one blue, one white, one yellow. He's puzzled.
The demon says, Take them to the caliph.
And I decided, yes, that's good enough:
she gets to live another day. I flipped
the pages eagerly. What next? What next?
And, lucky Andrew, Baptist boy, he read,
he made the trip to Mecca, he met the caliph.

CRIME AND PUNISHMENT

for Randy Rhoda

I close the book on *Crime and Punishment*
And think of you, my friend, the gifted student,
Who switched your major, once at M.I.T.,
To history, then anthropology—
Through half the catalogue in seven years,
First in, then out of school, grinding your gears.
Playing Raskolnikov, your plight became
Almost a joke between us. Now that name
Reminds me how the spiralling depression
That dragged you from confusion to confession
Blunted your gifts.
        For fourteen years of hard time
You stalked through Boston, but your only crime
Was killing your own future, spinning wheels
From Cambridge to the Back Bay's cobbled hills
Driving a taxi—or on all-night walks
Roaming the back streets, where, for several blocks,
You fled, one cold night, pounding the cement
Past stop sign, parked car, light, and tenement,
While steadily behind, a shadow gained,
Waving a pistol. When at last you turned
To face your nemesis, you met no double,
But a common thief, who cursed you for your trouble,
Rifling your wallet with, "What *is* this shit?
Just some goddamned IDs—go on, then, keep it,"
Then tossing back your life.
        So what's your crime?
What spins you down the sidewalk like a dime
Wobbling, wobbling . . . always just off-center

As autumn passes and approaching winter
Makes Boston your Siberia, your fate
The tragedy you lived to recreate
For me each summer, turning your life to art,
While I, who should have been your counterpart,
Kept both at a safe distance, and now write
What you said then with such criminal delight.

BLUE JAY

A sound like a rusty pump beneath our window
Woke us at dawn. Drawing the curtains back,
We saw—through milky light, above the doghouse—
A blue jay lecturing a neighbor's cat
So fiercely that, at first, it seemed to wonder
When birds forgot the diplomacy of flight
And met, instead, each charge with a wild swoop,
Metallic cry, and angry thrust of beak.

Later, we found the reason. Near the fence
Among the flowerless stalks of daffodils,
A weak piping of feathers. Too late now to go back
To nest again among the sheltering leaves.
And so, harrying the dog, routing the cat,
And taking sole possession of the yard,
The mother swooped all morning.

                                        I found her there
Still fluttering round my head, still scattering
The troops of blackbirds, head cocked toward my car
As if it were some lurid animal,
When I returned from work. Still keeping faith.
As if what I had found by afternoon
Silent and still and hidden in tall grass
Might rise again above the fallen world;
As if the dead were not past mothering.

Paul Lake

IN ROUGH WEATHER

for Steve

The storm blew up so suddenly,
cresting the hills, we just had time
to leave our hooks where they had caught
on the first cast, quickly cutting lines
and aiming our prow across the lake
to race the storm. Crouched in the hull,
I shouted directions while you fought,
with stuttering engine, swell after swell,
nosing our wave-clapped, drunken prow
into the whitecaps till it rang
or sipped at water in the troughs,
bellying to light. You timed each plunge
and kept us edging toward the shore
by starts—and when we took on water
and seemed, mid-lake, to stand stock-still,
you played big brother to your big brother,
steadying me with your steady skill.
And once, when we both thought we would flounder
and I looked back, we saw our fear
doubled by all that might go under—
and all that was dear was doubly dear.

INTRODUCTION TO POETRY

She comes in late, then settles like a sigh
On the first day, returning every week
Promptly at ten, each Monday Wednesday Friday,
To study Shakespeare, Jonson, Donne, and Blake;

Enters the room to an approving murmur,
Straightens her dress, then, brushing back her hair,
Arches her body with the slightest tremor,
And sits, while the room grows breathless, in her chair;

Sits for an hour, while busy sophomores worry
Each turgid line, a Botticellian smile
On her rapt face, who's learned how little study
Love involves; who, walking down the aisle,

Knows in her bones how little poetry
Words breathe, and how—on turning to go home—
All eyes will watch her rise above her "C"
And walk off, like a goddess on the foam.

THE FEUD

I don't know your stories. This one here
is the meanest one *I've* got or ever hope to.
Less than a year ago. Last of November,
but hot by God! I saw the Walker gang,

lugging a little buck. (A sandwich size.
It *would* be. That bunch doesn't have the patience.
I'd passed up two no smaller, and in the end
the family had no venison that fall.)

I waved to them from the porch—they just looked up—
and turned away. I try to keep good terms
with everyone, but with a crowd like that
I don't do any more than necessary.

It wasn't too much cooler back inside.
A note from my wife on the table said the heat
had driven her and the kids to the town pond beach
to sit. That made some sense. It's the last that will.

I peeked out quick through the window as the Walkers'
truck ripped past, and said out loud, "Damn fools!"
The old man, "Sanitary Jim" they call him,
at the wheel, the rifles piled between

him and "Step-and-a-Half," the crippled son.
In back, all smiles and sucking down his beer,
"Short Jim" and the deer. Now Short Jim seems all right.
To see his eyes, in fact, you'd call him shy.

He doesn't talk quite plain. Each word sounds like
a noise you'd hear from under shallow water.
I didn't give it too much thought till later,
when the wife and kids came home, and wanted to know

what in Jesus' name that awful smell was,
over the road? Turns out that Walker crew
had left their deer guts cooking in the sun.
And wasn't that just like them? Swear to God,

to leave that mess beside a neighbor's house
for stink, and for his dogs to gobble up?
And there was one thing more that puzzled me:
why wouldn't they take home that pile of guts

to feed *their* dogs? A worthless bunch—
the dogs, I mean, as well as them. You'd think
they wouldn't be above it. Every decent
dog they ever had was bullshit luck,

since every one they run is one they stole
or mooched out of the pound. You'll see them all,
hitched to one lone post, dung to the elbows,
and every time they get themselves a new one,

he'll have to fight it out until the others
either chew him up or give him up.
I guessed I'd do this feeding for them, so
I raked up all the lights into a bag

and after nightfall strewed them in their dooryard
with a note: "Since I'm not eating any deer meat,
I'd just as quick your guts rot somewhere else
as by my house." And signed my actual name.

The whole thing's clear as Judgment in my mind:
the sky was orange, the air so thick it burned

a man out of his senses. I'm the one.
And evening never seemed to cool me off,

though I'm a man whose aim is not to truck
in such a thing. I've lost most of my churching,
but don't believe in taking up with feuds.
I usually let the Good Lord have His vengeance.

Nothing any good has ever grown
out of revenge. So I was told in school
when I slapped up Lemmie Watson, because he broke
the little mill I built down on the brook.

And so I learned. I spent the afternoons
that week indoors, and I've been different since,
till this one day. Then something else took over.
There passed a week: they stove my mailbox up.

At least I don't know who in hell beside them
would have done it. I had a spare. (The Lord
knows why.) I cut a post and put it up,
and could have left the blessed fracas there,

and would have, as my wife advised me to.
And I agreed. I told myself all night,
my eyes wide open, lying there and chewing,
"Let it go." And would have, as I claim,

but two days passed, and they came hunting coons
on this side of the ridge. I heard their hounds.
(God knows what *they* were running. Hedgehogs? Skunks?
It could have been.) Out on the porch,

I heard *tick-tick*. Dog paws, and all *my* dogs
began to yap and whine. I made a light.
Shaky, thin as Satan, a docktail bitch,
a black-and-tan (almost), was looking in.

I made of her. She followed me as if
I'd owned her all my life out to the kennel.
I stuck her in the empty run that was
Old Joe's before I had to put him down.

I filled a dish with meal. She was a wolf!
The first square feed she'd had in quite a time.
My wife kept asking what I could be up to.
Likes to worry. Next day I drove clear

to Axtonbury, to the county pound.
"This dog's been hanging round my house all week.
Don't know who she belongs to." Lies, of course.
I had her collar locked in the Chevy's glovebox.

I wouldn't harm a dog unless I had to,
and figured this one stood a better show
to make out at the pound than at the Walkers'.
But the Walkers didn't know that. Driving home,

I flung the collar in their dooryard. After dark,
and spitting snow, six inches by next day,
late in December now, toward Christmas time.
Things shifted into higher gear despite me.

Or on account of me. Why not be honest?
I know that nowadays it's not the fashion
to think a person's born what he becomes;
but Sanitary Jim, his wife and family:

I never gave it too much thought but must
have figured right along that they belonged
to that great crowd of folks who *don't* belong.
Their children wear their marks right on them: speech

you hardly understand, a rock and sway
where a normal boy would take an easy stride.

And in and out of jail. If they can't find
another bunch to fight with, why, they'll fight

with one another. (Sleep with one another
too, if talk can be believed. Somehow
two homely sisters are in the mix as well.)
Short Jim beat an uncle or a cousin

—I disremember—beat him right to death.
(It's not the fashion either nowadays
to keep a violent man in jail. A month, no more,
goes by, and Short Jim's on the town again.)

But back to what I just began. The Walkers
are as bad as banty roosters, and I figured
they were meant somehow to be. Where most of us
are meant to eat one little peck of dirt,

they eat a truckload. Is it any wonder,
then, I didn't make a special point
of mixing with them? No more than I would
with any crowd that filthed itself that way.

But mix with them I did. It seemed as if
their style of working things reached up and grabbed me.
I was in the game so quick it turned my head.
The snow came on, the first big storm of winter,

that night I pulled the trick with the docktail's collar.
In the morning, barely filled, I saw their tracks
around my kennel. But *my* runs both are solid
chain-link, and the doors are padlocked shut.

They mean a thing or two to me, those dogs.
I keep the keys right on me. No one else
—no family, no good friend—can spring a dog
of mine. That way, I know they're there, or *with* me.

I'm only puzzled that they never growled. They do
as a rule. I was surely glad the Walkers hadn't
had the sense to bring along some poison.
A dog's a dog, which means he's five-eighths stomach.

Thinking on this gave me bad ideas.
But I'll get to that when time is right. For now,
I called myself a lucky fool, out loud,
and bolted both dogs shut inside their houses

nights. I judged this thing would soon blow over.
I burned a yardlight too, which I'd never done.
And that (I guessed) was the last they'd come past dark.
You know, the funny part of this whole battle

up to now, when you consider who
I'd got myself involved with, was that neither
side had come right out into the open.
The only thing I knew for sure they'd done

was leave a mess of guts out on my lawn.
The only thing for sure they knew of me—
that I returned that mess to its right home.
The mailbox and the collar and the tracks. . . .

For all we either knew, the Boss was making
visions in our eyes which, feeling righteous,
we took upon our *selves* to figure out.
And since, between the parties, I guessed *I*

had better claim to righteousness than they did,
I'm the one that—thinking back—began
to read the signs according to my will.
How many times have village hoodlums stove

a mailbox up? Or just plain village kids?
How many times, to mention what comes next,

has one old drunk shitkicker or another
raised some hell outside Ray Lawson's Auction

and Commission Sales on Friday night? And still,
I judged it was the Walkers who had slashed
all four of my new pickup's summer tires.
(Four months had passed.) And judged it quick as God.

The pickup spraddled like a hog on ice. It cost me
two hundred dollars just to run it home.
Next day I passed Short Jim as he came out
of Brandon's store and sized him up, and looked

at him: a man who'd killed another man,
but shyness in his eyes. He looked away.
And if *I'd* looked away just then. . . . Instead,
I saw a basket full of winter apples,

Baldwins mostly, full of slush and holes.
No wonder Brandon had that crop on sale!
Four cents each was asking more than enough
for winter apples still unsold in April.

If the top one hadn't had a hole as big,
almost, as half a dollar. . . . By God, where
would we be now? But there it was, the hole,
and I got notions. Maybe fate is notions

that you might have left alone, but took instead.
I did. I bought that apple, and another
just for show. And a box of pellets, too—
more rat pellets than I ever needed,

more than I could stuff into that hole
and still have stay enough in the rotten skin
to hold them in enough to fool a hog
that he *had* an apple. Walkers' hog, I mean.

They penned her on the far side of the road
from where that firetrap shack of theirs was built.
I didn't set right out. That apple sat
as much as seven days up on a post

of metal in the shed, where even rats
—Lord! let alone my kids—could never reach it.
And it sat inside my mind. Especially nights.
Or say it burned, the while I cooled myself

—or tried to do, with every nerve and muscle—
in bed, and said the same thing over and over:
"Nothing good will ever grow from feuds."
And just to get the apple *out* of mind,

spoke such damn foolishness you never heard:
"Old Mother Hubbard," "Stars and Stripes Forever"
(tried to get the words of one to go
along with the rhymes and rhythms of the other).

Then went down that seventh night, as if it was
another person who was going down
inside the shed (because the person I
believed I was kept up the sermon: "Nothing

any good from any feud," and so on),
picked the apple down, and put it in
my pocket, and—the moon was full—began
the uphill climb across the ridge. To Walkers'.

Stopped for breath at height of land, I turned
to see the house, where everyone was sleeping,
wondered what they dreamed, and if their dreams
were wild as mine become when moon's like that—

they say there's nothing in it, but as God
will witness me, a full moon fills my head,

asleep or not, with every bad idea.
One spring, the moon that big, a skunk came calling

in the shed, and my fool tomcat gave a rush.
The smell was worse than death. It woke me up,
if I was sleeping (I'd been trying to),
and till the dawn arrived, for hours I felt

the stink was like a judgement: every sin
from when I was a child till then flew back
and played itself again before my eyes.
High on the ridge, I felt I might reach out

and touch that moon, it was so close, but felt
that if I reached it, somehow it would burn.
It was a copper color, almost orange,
like a fire that's just beginning to take hold.

Your mind plays tricks. You live a certain while
and all the spooky stories that you read
or hear become a part of memory,
and you can't help it, grown or not, sometimes

the damnedest foolishness can haunt you. Owls,
for instance. I know owls. How many nights
do they take up outside, and I don't think
a thing about it? *That* night, though,

a pair began close by me. I'd have run,
the Devil take me, if the light had been
just one shade brighter, I'd have run right home
to get out of the woods or else to guard

the house, the wife, the kids. I don't know which.
A rat or mouse would shuffle in the leaves
and I would circle twenty yards around it.
I was close to lost until I found the brook

and waded it on down. It was half past two.
The moon kept working higher till I saw
the hog shed just across the road from Walkers' house.
There wasn't that much difference in the two.

I'm a man can't stand a mess. But they,
the boys and Sanitary Jim. . . . Well, they
can stand it. Seems that that's the way
that they *prefer* it. That hovel for the pig

was made of cardboard, chimney pipe, and wanes.
They'd driven I don't know how many sections
of ladder, side by side, into the mud
for fencing. Come the thaw each year, the ground

will heave that ladder up, and then you'll find
a pig in someone's parsnips. Anyway,
I looked the matter over, and the worry
that I'd felt about the thing that I was doing—

well, it went away. I felt as pure
as any saint or choirboy hunkered there.
I crept up on my knees and clapped the gate
(a box spring from a kid's bed) so the pig

would have a peek. I don't know why, exactly,
but I felt like watching as she took the apple
from my hand. It wouldn't do to leave it.
She just inhaled it, didn't even chew.

I backed up to the brook and watched some more,
then stepped in quick, because that poison sow
began to blow and hoot just like a bear.
The job was done. I hadn't left a track.

I don't know just what you'll make of this:
I fairly marched back up across the ridge

as if I made that climb four times a day.
The air was cold and sweet and clear, the way

it is when you can see the moon so plain.
I walked on to a beat and sang the hymns
—or sang them to myself—I'd got by heart
so many years before: "Old Rugged Cross"

and "Onward Christian Soldiers" and "Amazing
Grace," and never noticed how the cold
had numbed my feet till I was back in bed.
No one woke up. I slept two righteous hours.

You jump into a feud, and every tricks'
like one more piece of kindling on the fire.
That's how I think of it, and you'll see why.
Come evening of the next day, I was sick.

You don't go paddling nighttimes in a brook
in April, and expect it's just a trick.
All night it felt like someone had a flatiron
and kept laying it between my shoulder blades.

My feet and legs were colored like old ashes.
My throat was sore enough I couldn't speak.
My wife, who didn't have a small idea
of where I'd been beside beneath the quilts,

lay it all to how I carried on.
"You've heard the old expression, 'sick with worry.'
That's what you've brought yourself, I think, from scheming
on those godforsaken Walkers." She was right,

but not the way she thought she was. In time,
there wasn't any use, I had to go
down to the clinic, twenty miles away.
You know those places: wait there half a day,

then let them pound you, scratch their heads, and scratch
some foolishness on a scrap of paper, wait
the other half while the druggist dubs around
to find the thing he's after. Come home poor.

If it was only poor that I came home!
I drove through town at fifteen miles an hour.
Swear to God I couldn't wheel it faster,
the way I was. It was a job to push

the throttle down, and I could scarcely see,
so blinked my eyes a time or two when I reached
the flat out by the pond. Above the ridge
the sky was copper-orange, and thick black smoke

was flying up to heaven, straight as string.
I thought I felt the heat. (But that was fever.)
By Jesus, that was *my* house. "Chimney fire,"
I said out loud, or loud as I could talk,

my throat ached so. The words were just a whisper,
and they sounded wrong the minute they came out.
I felt like I would die from all this sickness.
They called me "walking wounded" at the clinic:

pneumonia, but just barely, in one lung;
but now I felt my blood would burst the skin
and I'd just up and die inside that truck.
I squinched my eyes and lay the throttle on.

I meant to do some good before I died.
My wife was wrestling with a metal ladder
that had sat outside all winter, though I'd meant
to get it under cover every day.

I used it cleaning chimneys. It was stuck
in puddle ice beside the western wall.

I jumped out of the truck before it stopped,
and fell, and got back up, sweet Christ,

I tried to run, and every step I took
was like a step you take in dreams, the space
from road to house seemed fifteen thousand miles.
I stumbled to the shed and grabbed an ax

and put it to the ground to free the ladder,
but the ground just wouldn't give the damned thing up,
and every lick was like I swung the ax
from under water. I had no more force

than a kid or cripple. *My* kid, meanwhile, cried
from behind a big storm window, "Daddy? Daddy?"
It sounded like a question. I gave up
and tried to call back up to him. I couldn't.

My words were nothing more than little squeaks,
and when they did come out, they were not plain.
And so my wife began to call the boy,
"Throw something through the window and jump out!"

He threw a model boat, a book, a drumstick.
He couldn't make a crack. I flung the ax.
It missed by half a mile. I threw again
and broke a hole, and scared the boy back in.

That was the last I saw him. Like a woman
sighing, that old house huffed once and fell.
Out back, beside the kennel, our baby daughter
danced and giggled to hear the howling dogs.

I went into dead faint. And Hell could come
for all of me. And that is what has come.
Thirty years gone by since Lemmie Watson
broke my little mill of sticks and weeds

down by the brook, and I kicked the tar from him
and stayed indoors all week when school let out.
And Mrs. What's-Her-Name, I disremember,
fussing at her desk, would shake her head

and ask out loud if one small paddle wheel
was worth all this? I had to answer No.
I had to write it down, "No good can grow
from any feud." I wrote it fifty times

each afternoon. And then one afternoon
the Walker crew lay down a string of guts
across the road. . . . The part of life you think
you've got done living lies in wait like Satan.

For me, it was revenge. And what to do
right now? The house is gone, the boy, and I
believe I know just how they came to be.
But do I? Do I know what led to what

or who's to blame? This time I'll let it go.
No man can find revenge for a thing like this.
They say revenge is something for the Lord.
And let Him have it. Him, such as He is.

THE WRONG WAY WILL HAUNT YOU

(Shooting a hound)

Spittle beads as ice along
her jaw on this last winter day.
And when I lift her, all her bones
are loose and light as sprigs of hay.

For years her wail has cut the woods
in parts, familiar. Hosts of hares
have glanced behind as she ploughed on
and pushed them to me unawares.

Now her muzzle skims the earth
as if she breathed a far dim scent,
and yet she holds her tracks to suit
my final, difficult intent.

For years with gun in hand I sensed
her circle shrinking to my point.
How odd that ever I should be
the center to that whirling hunt.

Here a yip and there a chop
meant some prime buck still blessed with breath,
and in the silences I feared
she'd run him to her own cold death.

The snow that clouds my sights could be
a trailing snow, just wet and new
enough to keep a scent alive,
but not so deep that she'd fall through.

She falls without a sound. Her blood
runs circular upon the ground.
I lug her to those thick strange woods
where she put our first hare around.

I kick a drift-top over her
(the hardpan won't accept my spade).
The wind makes up a howl as in
all cold old ballads on The Grave.

TELESCOPE

Light projected lifetimes ago
from farthest stars is arriving now
here where my poor house moans
on its chilling sills and stones;
and where I—quieter, sleepless,
with only my half-blind dog for witness,
everyone else in slumber—
stand silent before such wonders.
I know alone, and inexactly,
the inexact science of memory.
A man who studies things to come
for livelihood tells me in time
there will be a lens which, pointed back
to earth, may show us all our past,
even to our creation.
How little would be the elevation
it needed to show me the people
and places I might have considered crucial:
my young friend Michael drunkenly
hulking over his purple Harley,
rumbling murder in my driveway,
swearing against the blossoms of May
that pinkly dropped around us there
like what we might have taken for flares
of warning, if he had been less proud,
and I more equal to warning. I stood
dumb as a dog. You could call it collusion,
or guilt by reason of inaction.
With the glass I could also see the feathers
flare on a pheasant held by my father,

and the Springer who cocked her head and chattered,
and wanted to hunt, and what was the matter?
Around us the last of afternoon fell
on the last stalks standing in autumn fields
as now, by word and heart, he petitioned
me for the slightest recognition.
I wouldn't hear the argument.
I had no interest in what was meant,
his words kept rising into balloons
of white, like those things you see in cartoons
above a speaker's head.
Turn the lens a hair and he's dead,
mouth stone-rigid, heart gone bust.
And oh how slightly I'd have to adjust
the telescope in order to see
the woeful host of memory,
other scenes—not all of course
of life and death—that exact remorse:
the way a guttering candle flickers
—I simply don't know what to give her—
in the importuning eye of a girl;
my runt chum Ronnie in a whirl
of agony as I refrain
from choosing him up for some childhood team;
the whirling earth a galaxy
of scene and soul and silence and need.
A word or two, not much
beyond what I said . . . or a touch—
how little it seems it would have taken
to change the times I now imagine
in which a now quiet man or woman,
myself included, would come off better.
But all these moments are fixed forever,
and such a lens no more effective
than memory, no more corrective.

AT THE FLYFISHER'S SHACK

A structure, yes. You'd hardly say a house.
I say he loved it, though, the man who died here.
(In truth he seemed to pay it small attention.)
I find a blue-dun hackle neck he used,
some orange fur he pilfered from a kitten,
a tying bobbin hanging from its thread there,
a vise that held his hooks, the verdigris
collecting now where silver plate once was.
  A cap. A pair of boots. Impressions, these,
of his career, or were they first suggestions
of its end?
                  Outside, a great tree bends,
a pine that drew the children whose amusements
wrought the dips and swerves its branches show,
town kids whose absence I might call a function
of how the pine grows old with grace. Just so,
the old man's pain (and always there was plenty—
the son collapsed on a baseball field at twenty,
the grandson whom he raised who shot himself:
  always there was plenty. . . .). Pain also
might seem a part of what he chose from life,
a wage. He bent a little,
                    then a little
more. I see in mind the nose that dropped
toward the fly he tied, and ever nearer
every season; clear as tears, a bauble
gathers at its tip. I know this ought
to be grotesque or droll, and is and isn't.
He couldn't wipe it off, in concentration
rapt, in study, building something fine—

ephemeral, he knew, mere fur and feather.
Was this man good? Like us he was and wasn't.
He'd tie a half a dozen,

                    then would choose
two or maybe three that struck him right.
The cabin kept on falling all around,
but I am here to say the man could tie
whenever he'd a mind! And then he died,
the way we do. At least there's one sure truth.
A basket that he wove of brown ash roots
still holds hooks he wrapped and then unchose.

    I meant to speak of nothing but the chosen.
And yet they speak as well, all the unchosen
such distinction

                  —keen in mind—now blurred
like any other. How he'd criticize
the work of his own hand or of another's!
"But it comes down, I guess, to presentation.
Boy," he'd often tell me, "there are days
a bungled pattern's just what they prefer."
A little breeze now lisps its way downriver,
intent or not to shake the old pine's limbs.

    Woven, it appears, of very air,
inside the old friend's closet there's a coat.
Was it too much in vogue

                or not enough?
His family's photos peer unclear through dust;
I wonder what impression they have here.
His bobbin swings along its vague ellipse.
The chosen and unchosen: flies or lives;
  obsessions; patterns; things put on or not;
paths of sure intent

              or otherwise.

CLOUDED EVENING, LATE SEPTEMBER

Confusion of song. On the radio,
"The autumn leaves drift by my window."
      "Ba-ba, black sheep, have you any wool?"—

Over his crib, the mobile's tune.
And tumbling into the tub I fill,
      Sh sh: persistent rush of water.

His mother's away. Does her milk rush down?
She's away. *Sh sh*—persistent, I proffer
      A hush. I imagine her pained expression,

The way she folds her slender arms
To cover the stain. The child's all vision,
      All eyes in his blurry focus upon

Drifting stars and beasts of wool
Above his bed in their quiet collisions.
      "The autumn leaves of red and gold . . .

"I see her face, the summer kisses,
The sunburned hands I used to hold."
      The fall is sudden, real, cold.

And suddenly too my eyes are filled
With whatever it is that seems bound to tumble.
      I lift the child, who splashes and babbles,

As foolish there in scented water
As yesterday his older sister,
      Begging to swim past dusk in a lake.

Rocky, frigid, dark as ocean.
Soon The Bear and The Bull and Orion
    Would gallop over, the sky all flaked

With their brilliance. I wondered if I might save her
Should a wave come rushing down, wind-driven.
    Mere child herself, she yet imagines

Me of all people to be a master.
Harvest of song in late September:
    One for the little girl; one for my dame

(How is it that *absence* can crowd the brain?);
One for the infant who pukes and mewls;
    And one somehow adrift in clouds,

Like softest wool all gathered round.
Like softest wool, indeed, but full
    Of something bound to tumble down.

INSOMNIA: THE DISTANCES

Cliché can be true: You hate to open the paper
and read that someone stood,
      as dumb as wood,
    while a big truck knocked the plain hell out of her daughter
the morning after the party, as the child tried out
    her birthday bike. You can almost hear a lot
of scrambled sounds, and then the terrible quiet.
    Speaking of hell, how about the roar

    of air and people for thousands of feet before
the doomed plane crashes?
      Vacation clothes—madras,
    pastel, batik—bleed together, swear.
Bunches of people! Or the other scores that go down
    under official or unofficial guns
every day. Boom! Somebody's done,
    done in again—wiped out, dispatched. Or else

    just thrown back on him-or-her Self
by bad news; illness; violence:
      nothing but silence,
    except for tick and tock from a bedroom shelf,
or maybe the kitchen fridge's strange little moan,
    or the wires way out on the road—*click hum*—
like a too-hard-driven car as it cools down.
    Or a roofbeam groans. Maybe an apple falls,

    thump! on the lawn. Even that may cause
a person to muse:
      something can fall on you.

Don't feel safe because it never has.
"In this life, you'd better by God trust nothing":
    that's what I heard from a man of apparent learning,
in a cramped bar. (The Optimists were meeting
    in the main room). As if there were somehow

    another life. That was real. He knew.
I don't know how he knew it,
    but you could *see* it—
maybe in the way his bull neck bowed,
and the way he couldn't manage to keep the stammer
    out of his talk; his hands were like 8-pound hammers,
but they shook on his mug of beer. An end to the matter:
    that single comment. Then silence. Don't believe

    each and every thing you happen to read,
they say. All well-and-good,
    but when you-know-what
has hit the fan for someone you can see. . . .
That's different, and maybe then you begin to hear
    something behind what you read, like the indistinct words
of a far-off song. Don't ask me, How can we care
    about someone or something we don't even know?

    Listen to things. Color them in. Like so:
Somebody's saddened,
    she wants to know what'll happen—
charity's failing because the economy's slow.
What of a worthy cause like the Animal Shelter?
    I came on these worries a while back in a letter
to the editor: it could have been written better,
    but here that isn't my particular worry.

    She cares, though—about the kittens and puppies . .
"Where will they turn?"
    I'm afraid by now she's learned:
Down. So think of her. Maybe she fancies

a tricolor male, a "money cat," or a Manx.
      Something rare. A weird mutt, a mix
of skinny Bluetick hound and pedigreed Spitz,
      and so the pup has the nailkeg head of a Husky

      on top of a long-leg, racehorse body,
with markings by Heinz:
            57 stripes
      and spots. Or just a common pooch or tabby,
and all they do, and all she does, is whine.
      She can't speak, just lets the tears run down
till all are asleep. Common or garden pain:
      The child's hair was yellow, the bike was green,

      the sky was gray. . . . Was. That great big man,
the one at the bar:
            he was himself, sure,
      but also anybody whose life turns mean
as hell—maybe someone got shot, maybe
      something burned down; it's the end, maybe,
of a love they thought would last forever; or he
      —or needless to say it could be she—was

      supposed to be in the best of health. Was.
Supposed. There I was
            myself, supposed
      to be having the time of my life inside the walls
of this ruined Italian village. Quaint. Hell!
      no newspaper, books, not even any mail
to read for weeks. I still can't tell
      what it was: the tick of my little alarm!

      an animal's cry? Maybe a truck-tire's boom,
or a jet's; or a fridge that squeaked;
            or a rafter that creaked.
      Was someone somewhere singing a drunken song?
Or was it just this terrible quiet in the room,

and outside too?—Nothing. Not a peep.
And I woke up, and thought, and wrote this down,
in the night, in a tiny, silent, faraway town.

And now it seems a hell of a distance to sleep.

POST-COITUM TRISTESSE:
A SONNET

Why
do
you
sigh,
roar,
fall,
all
for
some
hum-
drum
come
—mm?
Hm . . .

THE HAUNTED

A crying white candle
    Lights the room where
The moon's fairest woman
    Brushes her hair
And we who are dying
    Just to be near her,
Who inextricably
    Adore and fear her,

Hurl ourselves flatly
    On the walls and floor,
Dancing a love-dance
    More and more
Frenzied until—a kind
    Of kiss—she places
Her mouth to the flame, and
    Blows out our faces.

THE GHOST OF A GHOST

I

The pleasures I took from life
were simple things—to play catch
in the evenings with my son,
or tease my daughter (whom I addressed
as Princess Pea), or to watch
television, curled on the floor.
Sometimes I liked to drink too much,
but not too often. Perhaps best
of all was the delight I found
waking to a drowse at one
or two at night and my wife
huffing (soft, not quite a snore)
beside me, a comforting sound.

We had our problems of course,
Emily and I, occasions when
things got out of hand.—Once she threw
a juice glass at me that broke
on the wall (that night I drew
a face there, a clownish man
catching it square on the nose,
and Emily laughed till she cried).
It's true I threatened divorce
a few times (she did too), but those
were ploys, harmless because love ran
through every word we spoke—
and then, an accident, I died.

II

Afterwards, my kids began
having nightmares—when they slept
at all; Emily moved in a haze,
looking older, ruined now, and wept
often and without warning.
The rooms had changed, become mere
photographs in which my face
was oddly missing . . . That first year
without me: summer twilight, and those
long leaf-raking Saturdays
without me, and Christmas morning—
the following August a new man,
a stranger, moved in and took my place.

You could scarcely start to comprehend
how queer it is, to have your touch
go unfelt, your cries unheard
by your family. Princess!—I called—
Don't let that stranger take your hand!
And—*Em, dear, love, he has no right*
to you.
                    Where did they think I'd gone?
who walked the house all day, all night,
all night. It was far too much
for anyone to endure, and,
hammered by grief one ugly dawn,
I broke. I am still here!—I bawled
from the den—Still here! And no one stirred.

But in time I learned a vicious trick,
a way of gently positing
a breath upon a person's neck
to send an icy run of fear
scampering up the spine—anything,
anything to show them who was near!

. . . Anything, but only to retrieve
some sense that nothing is more
lasting than the love built week by week
for years; I had to believe
again that these were people I'd
give everything, even a life, for.
Then—a second time, and slow—I died.

III

Now I am a shadow of my
former shadow. Seepage of a kind
sets in. Settled concentrations thin.
Amenably—like the smile become
a pond, the pond a mud-lined
bed, from which stems push, pry
and hoist aloft seed-pods that
crack into a sort of grin—
things come almost but not quite
full circle; within the slow
tide of years, water dilutes to light,
light to a distant, eddying hum . . .
In another time, long ago,

I longed for a time when I'd
still felt near enough to recall
the downy scrape of a peach skin
on my tongue, the smell of the sea,
the pull of something resinous.
By turns, I have grown other-wise.
I move with a drift, a drowse that roams
not toward sleep but a clarity
of broadened linkages; it's in
a state wholly too gratified
and patient to be called eagerness
that I submit to a course which homes
outward, and misses nothing at all.

OLD BACHELOR BROTHER

Here from his prominent but thankfully
uncentral position at the head of the church—
a flanking member of the groom's large party—
he stands and waits to watch the women march

up the wide aisle, just the way they did
at last night's long and leaden-joked rehearsal.
Only this time, it's all changed. There's now a crowd,
of course, and walls of lit stained glass, and Purcell

ringing from the rented organist,
and yet the major difference, the one
that hits his throat as a sort of smoky thirst,
is how, so far away, the church's main

doors are flung back, uncovering a square
of sun that streams into the narthex, so that
the women who materialize there
do so in blinding silhouette,

and these are not the women he has helloed
and kissed, and who have bored, ignored, or teased him,
but girls—whose high, garlanded hair goes haloed
by the noon-light . . . The years have dropped from them.

One by one they're bodied forth, edged with flame,
as new as flame, destined to part the sea
of faces on each side, and approaching him
in all their passionate anonymity.

THE SHADOW RETURNS

Saw my shadow on the wall,
Saw my shadow, saw it fall
And renew itself with light.

It was my death that stung my sight:
Substantial time to race my heart
Before I turned from it in doubt.

It was my love upon the bed
Who pointed out my silhouette,
Anonymous and monochrome.

Never understood, till then,
The subtle bond of ghost and kin,
The visible world invisibles win.

Into the evening far sounds came,
Like laughter of people after tea
Rising to brush the crumbs away—

They always sounded false and thin,
Almost evil, estranged from pain,
But now this sound was part of me
And I was part of the world again.

A MEETING OF FRIENDS

Although their hair is turning gray
     They're tall and blue:
A white silk scarf, a strain of Bach
     Is what is new.

The beautiful now calmly shines
     Where once it fled,
The terror of their innocence
     Is almost dead.

They meet for lunch this time of year
     And always find
The brightness that their boyhood held
     Not far behind;

And though the distance that they keep
     Estranges others,
They share a dark, unsettled plain
     Like brothers.

When does a life begin to form
     And carry out
A silent vow the tongue cannot
     Articulate:

A line that travels, wavers, breaks,
     And then returns
As if the changes surfacing
     Were in the plans.

Why speak of men who look so glad
    And know their worth,
Settling inside their lives
    This side of death—

Have I been sent to sit all day
    And figure out
The true relations flickering
    Between two hearts?

Or do the truest feelings
    Lie on this leaf,
Where stories fit together,
    Unfolding grief.

One always holds a few words back,
    The other smiles;
Smoke curls through music as they talk
    Of work and miles;

For still they save what is not said
    Until the end,
When things untold turn into things
    Never meant.

On the border of the future
    Broods the infinite:
There knowledge slowly sips her wine
    And savors it.

But time is a stranger entering
    Without a sound,
And love is a stream changing course
    Underground.

THE LOST BEE

As a lost bee returning to the hive . . .
Allen Tate

When I returned to the hive I was one
Among many, in a blistering hum.
A braid of air had brought me far from home
—Blinder than flowers, simpler than the sun,

Weaving through waves of incandescent curves
That offered what they always had to give.
Then why suddenly did the hive seem a grave,
The queen, in her mystery, an end to serve

Who before was my mother, my god?
What happened on the way, and how did I lose
Direction, season, aim—scanning the skies
Numbly for a current, a sequence, a strand.

They welcomed me back with a typical dance,
But its fantastic patterns made no sense;
And yet I know, now, a tempo that encodes
The temples and fields, the pulse of time and space.

I must have been exiled from habit
By a strange wind, a stray leaf, a migration
Constellating unheard-of combinations;
But they don't notice, they don't mention it.

Their honey is too sweet, the hive too dark,
The swarm of cells too tight; and who can I tell
Or fly with?—for nothing we make can seal
The knowledge vaulting outside the matriarch.

In the flurry and buzz of business meetings
All that we hear is a forecast of trouble:
The comb's overcrowded, the queen's gold bubble
Polluted by pollen clouding her wings.

She's laid plans for starting a new colony
To restore our nectar's profit and destroy
The sting of death, decay, and anarchy.
Our empire's estate of wax and honey

Will thrive again, one day; and it is rumored
That I have been destined to attend
The queen on her odyssey—she trusts me,
Or perhaps she has grown sick of loyalty.

NIGHT COACH

From the window of a train
The moon appears and flees,
A brilliant silent film
Cut up by winter trees.

A child approaching two
Wakes mother from her nap
And crawls onto my lap
To get a better view.

Breaking into speech
She taps the windowpane:
This is the first full moon
That she will try to reach.

Seated across the aisle
Man and woman smile
At infant in papoose;
A Mediterranean face

Bends over it and coos,
"Bambino, little one"—
The beautiful, foreign
Father a child would choose.

Kindness everywhere grows
In limited quantities,
But the borders close,
The fountains freeze,

And the brightest halo
Shrinks to a shadow
Gray as a noose.
Intangible truths

Vie with cruelty
For untranslatable bread.
Oh God, let us be free,
We call out to no god—

What else can be said
To sparse stars overhead,
Lighting up the home
Of a darker dark?

The train runs on its track.
Together and alone
The tossing sleepers moan;
Nothing answers back.

SATYR, CUNNILINGUENT:
TO HERMAN MELVILLE

1/

Twining her fingers through
His hair, fingertips drumming,
At last she brings him to
The sweet verge of her coming:

Her passion at its flood
Overwhelms all measure;
On articulation's bud,
Inarticulate with pleasure

She flops like a caught fish
Straining to be human.
This Satyr has his wish
Fulfilled in a mortal woman.

2/

Flesh is a mystery:
Had Billy a young bride
As Ahab had, would he
Not have been less tongue-tied?

Might he not have become
Glib in the face of darkness,
As you yourself in some
Moods seem to practice

The clever, tongue in cheek
Art of the cunning Satyr?
How hard it is to speak
Of things that matter.

SHARKS AT THE NEW YORK AQUARIUM

Suddenly drawn in through the thick glass plate
And swimming among them, I imagine
Myself as, briefly, part of the pattern
Traced in the water as they circulate
In sullen obedience to the few laws
That thread the needle of their simple lives:
One moment in a window of serrated knives,
Old-fashioned razors and electric saws.
And then the sudden, steep, sidewinding pass:
No sound at all. The waters turning pink,
Then rose, then red, after a long while clear.
And here I am again outside the tank,
Uneasily wrapped in our atmosphere.
Children almost never tap the glass.

Charles Martin

SPEECH AGAINST STONE

I watch a man in the schoolyard
As he brushes a flat coat of institutional beige
Over a wall brilliant with childish graffiti,
                    Turning a fresh page,

A surface the kids will respray
As soon as his back is turned. I suppose I should
Be thinking—as any upstanding, taxpay-
                    ing citizen would—

Of the money and man-hours spent
Covering up these phosphorescent hues
And adolescent cries of discontent;
                    But as he continues,

I find myself divided:
The huge roller goes sweeping on over the stone,
And I see in what he is doing a labor
                    Not unlike my own

When I erase, letter by letter,
The words I've just written, in the hope that all
My scratching out may summon something better—
                    And besides, the wall

Surely approves of this work,
For who can believe it would choose to say
FUCK THE WORLD or FAT ANTHONYS A JERK
                    Or DMF JOSE?

No, left to its own devices,
The wall would stand forever an unlettered book,
Prepared to meet eternity's inspection
                    With its own blank look.

        But that, of course, is what summons
The hidden children out of their hiding places—
That inviting blankness as the janitor finally covers
                    Up the last traces,

        Gathers together his painting
Gear and goes clattering off. No sooner gone
Than they return to renew the ancient complaint
                    Of speech against stone,

        Spelling out—misspelling, often—
The legends of the heart's lust for joy and violence
In waves that break upon but will not soften
                    The cliffs of obdurate silence.

Charles Martin

METAPHOR OF GRASS IN CALIFORNIA

The seeds of certain grasses that once grew
Over the graves of those who fell at Troy
Were brought to California in the hooves
Of Spanish cattle. Trodden into the soil,

They liked it well enough to germinate,
Awakening into another scene
Of conquest: blade fell upon flashing blade
Until the native grasses fled the field,

And the native flowers bowed to their dominion.
Small clumps of them fought on as they retreated
Toward isolated ledges of serpentine,
Repellent to their conquerors. . . .
                                        In defeat,

They were like men who see their city taken,
And think of grass—how soon it will conceal
All of the scattered bodies of the slain;
As such men fall, these fell, but silently.

E. S. L.

My frowning students carve
Me monsters out of prose:
This one—a gargoyle—thumbs its contemptuous nose
At how, in English, subject must agree
With verb—for any such agreement shows
Too great a willingness to serve,
A docility

Which wiry Miss Choi
Finds un-American.
She steals a hard look at me. I wink. Her grin
Is my reward. *In his will, our peace, our Pass:*
Gargoyle erased, subject and verb now in
Agreement, reach object, enjoy
Temporary truce.

Tonight my students must
Agree or disagree:
America is still a land of opportunity.
The answer is always, uniformly, *Yes*—even though
"It has no doubt that here were to much free,"
As Miss Torrico will insist.
She and I both know

That Language binds us fast,
And those of us without
Are bound and gagged by those within. Each fledgling polyglot
Must shake old habits: tapping her sneakered feet,
Miss Choi exorcises incensed ancestors, flout-

ing the ghosts of her Chinese past.
     Writhing in the seat

     Next to Miss Choi, Mister
     Fedakis, in anguish
Labors to express himself in a tongue which
Proves *Linear B* to me, when I attempt to read it
Later. They're here for English as a Second language,
     Which I'm teaching this semester.
     God knows they need it,

     And so, thank God, do they.
     The night's made easier
By our agreement: I am here to help deliver
Them into the good life they write me papers about.
English is pre-requisite for that endeavor,
     Explored in their nightly essays
     Boldly setting out

     To reconnoiter the fair
     New World they would enter:
Suburban Paradise, the endless shopping center
Where one may browse for hours before one chooses
Some new necessity—gold-flecked magenta
     Wallpaper to re-do the spare
     Bath no one uses,

     Or a machine which can,
     In seven seconds, crush
A newborn calf into such seamless mush
As a *mousse* might be made of—or our true sublime:
The gleaming counters where frosted cosmeticians brush
     Decades from the allotted span,
     Abrogating Time

As the spring tide brushes
A single sinister
Footprint from the otherwise unwrinkled shore
Of America the Blank. In absolute confusion
Poor Mister Fedakis rumbles with despair
And puts the finishing smutches
To his conclusion

While Miss Choi erases:
One more gargoyle routed.
Their pure, erroneous lines yield an illuminated
Map of the new found land. We will never arrive there,
Since it exists only in what we say about it,
As all the rest of my class is
Bound to discover.

EASTER SUNDAY, 1985

> To take steps toward the reappearance alive of the disap-
> peared is a subversive act, and measures will be adopted
> to deal with it.
> —*General Oscar Mejia Victores, President of Guatemala*

In the Palace of the President this morning,
The General is gripped by the suspicion
That those who were disappeared will be returning
In a subversive act of resurrection.

Why do you worry? The disappeared can never
Be brought back from wherever they were taken;
The age of miracles is gone forever;
These are not sleeping, nor will they awaken.

And if some tell you Christ once reappeared
Alive, one Easter morning, that he was seen—
Give them the lie, for who today can find him?

He is perhaps with those who were disappeared,
Broken and killed, flung into some ravine
With his arms safely wired up behind him.

VICTORIA'S SECRET

Victorian mothers instructed their daughters, ahem,
That whenever their husbands were getting it on them,
The only thing for it was just to lie perfectly flat
And try to imagine themselves out buying a new hat;
So, night after night, expeditions grimly set off
Each leaving a corpse in its wake to service the toff
With the whiskers and whiskey, the lecherous ogre bent
Over her, thrashing and thrusting until he was spent.
Or so we imagine, persuaded that our ancestors
Couldn't have been as free from repression as we are,
As our descendants will no doubt mock any passion
They think we were prone to, if thinking comes back into fashion.
And here is *Victoria's Secret*, which fondly supposes
That the young women depicted in various poses
Of complaisant negligence somehow or other reveal
More than we see of them: we're intended to feel
That this isn't simply a matter of sheer lingerie,
But rather the baring of something long hidden away
Behind an outmoded conception of rectitude:
Liberation appears to us, not entirely nude,
In the form of a fullbreasted nymph, impeccably slim,
Airbrushed at each conjunction of torso and limb,
Who looks up from the page with large and curious eyes
That never close: and in their depths lie frozen
The wordless dreams shared by all merchandise,
Even the hats that wait in the dark to be chosen.

BALANCE

He watch her like a coonhound watch a tree.
What might explain the metamorphosis
he underwent when she paraded by
with tea-cakes, in her fresh and shabby dress?
(As one would carry water from a well—
straight-backed, high-headed, like a diadem,
with careful grace so that no drop will spill—
she balanced, almost brimming, her one name.)

She think she something, stuck-up island bitch.
Chopping wood, hanging laundry on the line,
and tantalizingly within his reach,
she honed his body's yearning to a keen,
sharp point. And on that point she balanced life.
That hoe Diverne think she Marse Tyler's wife.

CHOPIN

It's Sunday evening. Pomp holds the receipts
of all the colored families on the Hill
in his wide lap, and shows which white store cheats
these patrons, who can't read a weekly bill.
His parlor's full of men holding their hats
and women who admire his girls' good hair.
Pomp warns them not to vote for Democrats,
controlling half of Hickman from his chair.
The varying degrees of cheating seen,
he nods toward the piano. Slender, tall,
a Fisk girl passing-white, almost nineteen,
his Blanche folds the piano's paisley shawl
and plays Chopin. And blessed are the meek
who have to buy in white men's stores next week.

THE BALLAD OF AUNT GENEVA

Geneva was the wild one.
Geneva was a tart.
Geneva met a blue-eyed boy
and gave away her heart.

Geneva ran a roadhouse.
Geneva wasn't sent
to college like the others:
Pomp's pride her punishment.

She cooked out on the river,
watching the shore slide by,
her lips pursed into hardness,
her deep-set brown eyes dry.

They say she killed a woman
over a good black man
by braining the jealous heifer
with an iron frying pan.

They say, when she was eighty,
she got up late at night
and sneaked her old, white lover in
to make love, and to fight.

First, they heard the tell-tale
singing of the springs,
then Geneva's voice rang out:
I need to buy some things,

So next time, bring more money.
And bring more moxie, too.
I ain't got no time to waste
on limp white mens like you.

Oh yeah? Well, Mister White Man,
it sure might be stone-white,
but my thing's white as it is.
And you know damn well I'm right.

Now listen: take your heart pills
and pay the doctor mind.
If you up and die on me,
I'll whip your white behind.

They tiptoed through the parlor
on heavy, time-slowed feet.
She watched him, from her front door,
walk down the dawnlit street.

Geneva was the wild one.
Geneva was a tart.
Geneva met a blue-eyed boy
and gave away her heart.

DESIRE

It doesn't speak and it isn't schooled,
like a small foetal animal with wettened fur.
It is the blind instinct for life unruled,
visceral frankincense and animal myrrh.
It is what babies bring to kings,
an eyes-shut, ears-shut medicine of the heart
that smells and touches endings and beginnings
without the details of time's experienced *part-
fit-into-part-fit-into-part.* Like a paw,
it is blunt; like a pet who knows you
and nudges your knee with its snout—but more raw
and blinder and younger and more divine, too,
than the tamed wild—it's the drive for what is real,
deeper than the brain's detail: the drive to feel.

THOSE PAPERWEIGHTS
WITH SNOW INSIDE

Dad pushed my mother down the cellar stairs.
Gram had me name each plant in her garden.
My father got drunk. Ma went to country fairs.
The pet chameleon we had was warden
of the living-room curtains where us kids
stood waiting for their headlights to turn in.
My mother took me to the library where ids
entered the Land of Faery or slipped in
the houses of the rich. A teacher told me
to brush my teeth. My sister ran away.
My father broke the kitchen table in half.
My mother went to work. Not to carry
all this in the body's frame is not to see
how the heart and arms were formed on its behalf.
I can't put the burden down. It's what formed
the house I became as the glass ball stormed.

HOW I COME TO YOU

Even a rock
has insides.
Smash one and see
how the shock

reveals the rough
dismantled gut
of a thing once dense.
Making the cut

into yourself,
maybe you hoped
for rock solid through.
That hope I hoped,

too. Dashed
on my rocks was my wish
of what I was. Angry,
dense and mulish,

I smashed myself
and found my heart
a cave, ready to be
lived in. A start,

veined, unmined.
This is how I come to you:
broken,
not what I knew.

DREAM COME TRUE

The little girl is shy.
She wonders why
on tiptoes, like paws,
there are laws

such as these:
she will never please
however much
she curtsies, never touch

except the dead head
she touches now and
springs away from, knocking
the flowers, ripping her stocking

on the casket that is
so much higher than she is.
She gets nothing
because there is nothing

but pale flowers on a waxed floor,
no more "Stop that!" then no more.
Her father who lies there
will be her nightmare.

THE WHEEL

Because of your nose, like a leaf blade
turned outward; because of the veins, also
leaflike, but stronger, surging up your forearms;
because of the moles spotting your arms
and neck and face like a long mottled animal;
because of the thrillingly perfect grades you made;
because no other girl had you (and I felt
you might want to be had) and beyond this felt
you would not refuse me, I made my play
at Junior Carnival, and threw myself at you
as if I'd done it a thousand times before
(and of course I had—I'd thrown myself away
on my parents' refusals), as if I knew
for certain you'd receive me at the door
of the side gymnasium, flattered, shy,
talking quickly back to me, leaning your shoulder
against the threshhold, me leaning closer,
smelling your laundered shirt, you not questioning why
I had chosen you, the one gripping the math folder,
gently accepting my self-exposure
(so needing acceptance yourself); because
of all this I ask you twenty-five years later
to be my husband and you ask me
to be your wife, our first wishes
confirmed at last as our best, spun out, original,
as if our lives were a novel ending (it really
makes sense you left math for literature) with kisses,
and from the games in the dim gymnasium, applause
as the frozen wheel of fortune thaws.

HAVE YOU EVER FAKED AN ORGASM?

When I get nervous, it's so hard not to.
When I'm expected to come in something
other than my ordinary way, to
take pleasure in the new way, lost, not knowing

how to drive it back to sureness . . . where are
the thousand thousand flowers I always pass,
the violet flannel, then the sharpness?
I can't, I can't . . . extinguish the star

in a burst. It goes on glowing. Your head
between my legs so long. Do you really
want to be there? I whimper as though . . .
then get mad. I could smash your valiant head.

"You didn't come, did you?" Naturally, you know.
Although I try to lie, the truth escapes me
almost like an orgasm itself. Then the "No"
that should crack a world, but doesn't, slips free.

THE RETURN

When I open my legs to let you seek,
seek inside me, seeking more, I think
"What are you looking for?" and feel it will
be hid from me, whatever it is, still
or rapidly moving beyond my frequency.
Then I declare you a mystery
and stop myself from moving and hold still
until you can find your orgasm. Peak
is partly what you look for, and the brink
you love to come to and return to must
be part of it, too, thrust, build, the trust
that brings me, surprised, to a brink of my own . . .
I must be blind to something of my own
you recognize and look for. A diamond
speaks in a way through its beams, though it's dumb
to the brilliance it reflects. A gem at the back
of the cave must tell you, "Yes, you can go back."

A WINTER'S TALE

for Ian

Silent and small in your wet sleep,
You grew to the traveler's tale
We made of you so we could keep
You safe in our vague pastoral,

And silent when the doctors tugged
Heels up your body free of its
Deep habitat, shoulders shrugged
Against the cold air's continent

We made you take for breathing,
Ian, your birth was my close land
Turned green, the stone rolled back for leaving,
My father dead and you returned.

INSOMNIA

Count the number of times boards crack
In a cooling house, or furniture plays
Like a thin percussionist tapping his way,
Working the bones over and back,
A blindman's stick or erratic clock,
The door that clicks in its frame as a key,
Which someone works in your lock
Without forcing it, works patiently.

TO BE SUNG ON THE FOURTH OF JULY

We come to this country
By every roundabout,
With hunger like a startled face
And passports folding doubt,

With leaving home as commonplace
As children waking clear,
And hopeful as a fishline cast
Deep from the harbor's pier

To the idea of a country,
The garden and the name,
And a government by language
Called the New Jerusalem,

Where the trees have figured upward
As much as shadowed down;
And when we stood beneath them
We hugely looked around,

Because our gift is figures
That turn along our thought,
The apple, rock, and water,
The ram suddenly caught—

A country of inheritors
Who only learn of late,
Who set their eyes as blankly
As their livestock stand and wait,

There where the markets gabble
Till the bell has rung them home,
There were Chicago barters
The wheat crop for a loan,

Wait like the Cuyahoga
Floating tons of oil,
A city's burning river
And Cleveland set for spoil,

Wait like the black lake barges
That punctuate the course
Or linger in ellipsis
Between the yawning shores . . .

And then that huge interior
That always seems the same,
Abandoned wells, neglected fields,
And immigrants who came

Mapping the land they traveled for,
Stayed, worked a while, then died,
Or moved to cities where
They also worked and died

As, settlers who burned and built
And surveyed every line,
We timbered, plowed, and harvested
To songs in three-four time.

Our figures are like fireworks,
And water turned to fire;
In Cleveland or Chicago
The people never tire

Of the ballads of an innocence
That would not be dissolved,

But burned the witch and stuck like tar . . .
To the first citizen ever saved.

And though at times in chorus,
The music almost right,
We sing away the darkness
That makes a window bright,

In fact we're born too lucky
To see a street's neglect,
For the years have pushed us next to
An unalike Elect—

Who say the lost are with us
The way our backs go bad
Or eyes require new glasses
To peer into what's sad,

Which occupies the TV set
And functions by contrast,
Because well-being needs a grief
To make the feeling last.

THE FERRIS WHEEL

The rounding steeps and jostles were one thing;
And he held tight with so much circling.
The pancaked earth came magnifying up,
Then shrank, as climbing backward to the top
He looked ahead for something in the fields
To stabilize the wheel.

Sometimes it stopped. The chairs rocked back and forth,
As couples holding hands got off
And others climbed into the empty chairs;
Then they were turning, singles, pairs,
Rising, falling through everything they saw,
Whatever thing they saw.

Below—the crowd, a holiday of shirts,
Straw hats, balloons, and brightly colored skirts,
So beautiful, he thought, looking down now,
While the stubborn wheel ground on, as to allow
Some stark monotony within,
For those festooned along the rim.

The engine, axle, spokes, and gears were rigged
So at the top the chairs danced tipsy jigs,
A teetering both balanced and extreme,
"Oh no," the couples cried, laughing, "Stop!" they screamed
Over the rounding down they rode along,
Centrifugal and holding on.

And he held too, thinking maybe happiness
Was simply going on, kept up unless

The wheel slowed or stopped for good. Otherwise,
There were the voices, expectant of surprise;
Funny to hear, he thought, their cries, always late,
Each time the wheel would hesitate,

Since the genius of the wheel was accident,
The always-almost that hadn't,
A minor agony rehearsed as fun
While the lights came up and dark replaced the sun,
Seeming to complete their going round all day,
Paying to be turned that way.

Later, standing off, he felt the wheel's mild dread,
Going as though it lapped the miles ahead
And rolled them up into the cloudless black,
While those who rode accelerated back
And up into the night's steep zero-G
That proved them free.

ELDERLY LADY CROSSING ON GREEN

And give her no scouts doing their one good deed
Or sentimental cards to wish her well
During Christmas time or gallstone time—
Because there was a time, she'd like to tell,

She drove a loaded V8 powerglide
And would have run you flat as paint
To make the light before it turned on her,
Make it as she watched you faint

When looking up you saw her bearing down
Eyes locking you between the wheel and dash,
And you either scrambled back where you belonged
Or jaywalked to eternity, blown out like trash

Behind the grease spot where she braked on you. . . .
Never widow, wife, mother, or a bride,
And nothing up ahead she's looking for
But asphalt, the dotted line, the other side,

The way she's done a million times before,
With nothing in her brief to tell you more
Than she's a small tug on the tidal swell
Of her own sustaining notion that she's doing well.

A NOTE OF THANKS

Wallet stolen, so we must end our stay.
Then, while checking out, the wallet reappears
With an unsigned note saying, "Please forgive me;
This is an illness I have fought for years,
And for which you've suffered innocently.
P.S. I hope you haven't phoned about the cards."
I wave the wallet so my wife will see.
Smiling, she hangs up, and smiling she regards
The broad array of others passing by,
Each now special and uniquely understood.
We go back to our unmade room and laugh,
Happily agreeing that the names for "good"
Are not quite adequate and that each combines
Superlatives we but rarely think.
For the next three nights we drink a better wine.
And every day we go back through to check
The shops, buying what before had cost too much,
As if now Christmas and birthdays were planned
Years in advance. We watch others and are touched
To see how their faces are a dead-panned
Generality, holding close
The wishes and desires by which we all are gripped.
All charities seem practical to us,
All waiters deserving of a bigger tip.
And, though we counter such an urge,
We start to think we'd like to meet the thief,
To shake the hand of self-reforming courage
That somehow censored a former disbelief.
Then we are home and leafing through the bills
Sent us from an unknown world of pleasure;

One of us likes cheap perfume; the other thrills
Over shoes, fedoras, expensive dinners;
There are massage parlors and videos,
Magazines, sunglasses, pharmaceuticals,
Long-distance calls, a host of curios,
Gallons of booze. . . . Only now we make our call.
But then, on hold, we go on sifting through
The mail till turning up a postcard view
Of our hotel. Flipping it and drawing blanks,
We read, "So much enjoyed my stay with you
I thought I ought to jot a note of thanks."

READING BEFORE WE READ,
HOROSCOPE AND WEATHER

My father laughing over the morning paper
Where the written world fell open on the funnies,
Manic sports, stalled politics . . . and where
The Horoscope said, "now," the Forecast, "sunny,"

He couldn't laugh enough, so skipped a page,
Then another, till the backdoor shut,
An engine turned, and I woke up his age
In the mirror of a gray no scissors cut.

He backed out of his pulling in at night
As light elbowed past an opened door, failing
Down six empty steps. Now a wall-switch bites
Blue sparks before the neon's billowing

Over another kitchen's white-on-white
Enameling; and now the sun is up
And climbing through the windows to a height
I follow out and off beyond the steep

Fence and trees to where the sky cuts flat
And blank as the paper spread in front of him,
My father then, waiting till I'd padded in, pulled out
My chair, inched up, and yawned that he begin.

Nothing is as funny now as then.
Still, when they rumple in, they bring his eyes
And mine, squinting and wet with laughing
Over the cracked, cracked up, sidewise, unwise

Stories that I read to them, telling how
We bend, break, wires shorting, knotting and strange;
Never as the Horoscope's predicted "now,"
But as the weather comes, fresh and ignorant of change.

WELCOME TO HIROSHIMA

is what you first see, stepping off the train:
a billboard brought to you in living English
by Toshiba Electric. While a channel
silent in the TV of the brain

projects those flickering re-runs of a cloud
that brims its risen columnful like beer
and, spilling over, hangs its foamy head,
you feel a thirst for history: what year

it started to be safe to breathe the air,
and when to drink the blood and scum afloat
on the Ohta River. But no, the water's clear,
they pour it for your morning cup of tea

in one of the countless sunny coffee shops
whose plastic dioramas advertise
mutations of cuisine behind the glass:
a pancake sandwich; a pizza someone tops

with a maraschino cherry. Passing by
the Peace Park's floral hypocenter (where
how bravely, or with what mistaken cheer,
humanity erased its own erasure),

you enter the memorial museum
and through more glass are served, as on a dish
of blistered grass, three mannequins. Like gloves
a mother clips to coatsleeves, strings of flesh

hang from their fingertips; or as if tied
to recall a duty for us, *Reverence
the dead whose mourners too shall soon be dead,*
but all commemoration's swallowed up

in questions of bad taste, how re-created
horror mocks the grim original,
and thinking at last *They should have left it all*
you stop. This is the wristwatch of a child.

Jammed on the moment's impact, resolute
to communicate some message, although mute,
it gestures with its hands at eight-fifteen
and eight-fifteen and eight-fifteen again

while tables of statistics on the wall
update the news by calling on a roll
of tape, death gummed on death, and in the case
adjacent, an exhibit under glass

is glass itself: a shard the bomb slammed in
a woman's arm at eight-fifteen, but some
three decades on—as if to make it plain
hope's only as renewable as pain,

and as if all the unsung
debasements of the past may one day come
rising to the surface once again—
worked its filthy way out like a tongue.

WHAT DO WOMEN WANT?

"Look! It's a wedding!" At the ice cream shop's
pristine picture window, the fortyish
blonde in the nice-mother shorts and top
stops short to raise two cones, one in each hand,
as if to toast the frothy blur of bride
emerging from St. Brigid's across the green.
"Mom," a boy answers, "I said I want a *dish*."
But this washes under her, while a well-matched band
of aqua-clad attendants pours outside
to laugh among fresh, buttonholed young men.

Young men . . . remember *them*? Her entourage
now is six boys, and she buys each one his wish.
When she peers up from her purse, the newlyweds
have sped away, and she notices at last,
on the littered steps of the Universalist
Society, some ten yards from St. Brigid's,
a rat-haired old woman in a camouflage
Army-Navy outfit, in whose pockets bulge
rags, or papers, and an unbagged beverage.
Looks like a flask of vodka. But no, it's dish-

washing liquid! It's Ivory, the household god.
The shape is clear from here: a voodoo doll,
headless, with the waist pinched, like a bride.
Poor thing—her dirty secret nothing worse
than the dream of meals to wash up after. While
what *she* most craves, standing at this font
of hope, the soda-fountain, with the boys
all eating hand-to-mouth, is not to miss
the thing that . . . well, it's hard to say; but what
she'd want, if we were given what we want.

SUMMER 1983

None of us remembers these, the days
when passing strangers adored us at first sight,
just for living, or for strolling down the street;
praised all our given names; begged us to smile...
you, too, in a little while,
my darling, will have lost all this,
asked for a kiss will give one, and learn
how love dooms us to earn
love once we can speak of it.

FROST AT MIDNIGHT

> For I was reared
> In the great city, pent 'mid cloisters dim,
> And saw nought lovely but the sky and stars.
> But *thou*, my babe! shalt wander like a breeze
> By lakes and sandy shores . . .
> —*Coleridge*

1.

His children tuckered out, tucked in (three girls
jammed in one bedroom, the boy in the only other),
and Elinor dozing where the dining room
would be if they'd had room, the "Yank from Yankville,"
as he liked to call himself, was wide awake.
It was midnight, on the fifteenth of September,
1912, and Frost was thirty-eight.
Tonight, he'd stay up late before the fire
in his Morris chair, as he often did, and write
to Susan Hayes Ward of *The Independent,*
who'd been the first to put his name in print.
Hard to believe that he, New Hampshire teacher
and half-hearted farmer, poet of little note,
just days before had boarded *The Parisian*
from Boston to Glasgow, then taken the train to London
with all of those now sleeping in his care.
Or that a tip from a retired policeman
(they knew no one in England, not a soul)
had led them to the village of Beaconsfield,
and a cottage called The Bungalow (or Bung Hole,
in the family lingo) for a monthly rent
of twenty dollars. Why were they here?

They'd flipped a coin.
Heads England, tails Vancouver—the nickel rose
silver like the moon from the Atlantic
they'd cross, sea-sick, to see it land again.
And now they lived behind a looming hedge
of American laurel, taller than any he
had seen at home. He wasn't here to pose
at Englishness, although the place was quaint,
all right: the muffin man had stepped
out of the nursery rhyme to walk their street
with the flypaper man; the knife-grinder; the man
who dangled pots and pans for sale from a wagon
drawn by a donkey. All this the children loved,
and Elinor might still fulfill her dream
sometime of sleeping under thatch. But no,
he hadn't come to write about such things.
At the bottom of his trunk the manuscripts
of some hundred poems waited to be sorted
into two books or three, and he'd write more
about the world he knew and had left behind.

His firstborn Elliott dead (his fault, he thought—
he'd called for the wrong doctor); later a daughter,
her mother's namesake, who lived not quite two days—
he wouldn't stop to brood on those troubles now.
Tonight his mood was defiant, even "aberrant,"
he wrote to Susan Ward. He'd "achieve something
solid enough to sandbag editors with."
After all, it was just a few miles from here
that Milton, in a cottage like this (shared
with *his* three daughters) finished *Paradise Lost.*
And a mile or two the other way that Gray,
redeemed by glory, lay in a country churchyard.
"To London town what is it but a run?"
he closed in singsong, adding he'd step out
to the yard, before bed, to watch the city lights
in the distance "flaring like a dreary dawn."

Not quite—but a visionary flourish?
A biographer named Walsh, who went to live
in The Bungalow long after, noted how
London remains some twenty-one miles off.
Equipped with a naked eye, then, Frost could never
have caught the faintest glimmer of the city.
But was this the night the first biographer
would write of as the turning point? The night
the poems were taken from the trunk and sorted
into the first of all the selves he left?
It was sometime in September or October.
Frost sat on the cold floor. From time to time,
he'd crumple a ball and toss it in the fire.
He saw, in the hearth, the lights of London blaze
each time he found a poem to sacrifice:
that way he ones he saved could shine the brighter.
Or it may be, as the curling pages turned
brilliant a fierce instant, then to ash,
he was thinking of the sallow leaves that fell
indifferently outside, beyond the laurel,
and was terrified of their unwritten message.
By October's end, the book was done and out,
typed by his eldest, Lesley; a Mrs. Nutt
(who shrugged "the day of poetry is past")
allowed she was nonetheless "disposed" to publish.
A Boy's Will. He'd left boyhood after all.

2.

As a boy might skip a stone across a pond,
skim over fifty-one Octobers, to
the President with the winning smile. He'll fall
in less than one month's time in the Dallas sun.
He comes to return the favor of a white-
maned legend, lionized past recognition.
Once, squinting in the glare, fumbling with pages

that seemed on fire, the poet had declaimed
by heart (though he misspoke the young man's name)
a poem to inaugurate The New Frontier.
Robert Frost is dead; a library in his honor
at Amherst College today is dedicated.
"He knew the midnight as well as the high noon,"
Kennedy says. And now the library shelves
behind him will begin to accrete their proof.
Shoulder to shoulder, books file in like soldiers
to settle the literary territory
of one who has been seen as saint and monster.

One story goes back to Derry, New Hampshire, years
before England. Lesley was six or so.
In the middle of the night, she was awakened
by her father, who conducted her downstairs,
her feet cold on the floor. At the kitchen table
her mother wept, face hidden in her hands.
It was then that Lesley spotted the revolver.
"Take your choice," Frost said, as he waved the thing
between himself and Elinor—a less bracing
alternative than a poem unwritten yet
would give between two roads in a yellow wood.
"Before morning," he warned, "one of us will be dead."

The child was returned to bed. And only after
she'd tucked him in the earth would her memory
be brought to light—or fixed, at least, in print.
Was it true? Or a vivid, fluttering scarf of nightmare?
It wrapped, somehow, around the family neck.
For it wasn't Lesley, but her brother Carol
who—whether or not the grisly tale was real—
rewrote it with his life. It was the ninth
of October, 1940; he was thirty-eight.
He'd kept his own boy, Prescott, up for hours
with talk of his failures as a poet-farmer;
of fears (but here the doctors would be wrong—

his wife lived on for more than fifty years)
that Lillian might not even last the night.
When Prescott drifted off, he took the shotgun
he'd bought for Lillian as a wedding gift
and went downstairs, before the sun could rise,
to turn it on himself.

                  Strange how in families
time seeps through all we do, so that the order
in which things happen seems to bow before
the dreamlike authority of metaphor.
Marjorie, the baby, dies in childbirth;
Elinor (who was "the unspoken half,"
Frost said, "of everything I ever wrote"—
if it wasn't true, one has no doubt he meant it)
is stricken at the heart while climbing stairs,
as if away from the scenes to come, when Carol
step by step descends flights of despair,
and Irma's mind unravels in and out
of the hospital. Time spirals to rearrange
events to show us something beyond change.

"Two things are sure," Carol's father had written
to Lillian in the midst of a world war
in which, he thought, a man might best have died
a soldier. "He was driven distracted by life
and he was perfectly brave." And yet he runs
his hand across more pages, as if to smooth
the mound of a new grave: Carol's mind
was one, he writes this time, with a "twist from childhood."
Think how, the year before, he'd raced through stop-signs:
his eyes veered "off the road ahead too often."

Now Frost is eighty-eight. He can see ahead.
Poet of chance and choice, who tossed a coin
but knew which side his bread was buttered on,
who said, "The most inalienable right of man

is to go to hell in his own way," here he is
in a hospital bed, a hell he hasn't made.
He has a letter from Lesley, who knows him for
the stubborn vanities and selfless gestures.
She knows, dear girl, the words to make him well,
if anything can make him well. She calls him
"Robert Coeur de Lion." Too weak to write,
he dictates a final letter back to her.
"You're something of a Lesley de Lion
yourself," he says, and he commends the children's
poems she's been working on. It's good
to have a way with the young. The old man
hasn't lost his knack, even in prose,
for giving the truth the grandeur of a cadence.
"I'd rather be taken for brave than anything else."

THE WARTBURG, 1521-22

where Luther hides for ten months after the Diet of Worms

The garden where he broods is like a riddle.
    The circle of the gravel walk,
The sundial which is stationed in the middle,
    A poppy on its hairy stalk:
These are like clues from which may be inferred
Imperatives of the Almighty's Word.

And nature veils, he thinks, a master plan.
    Where hunters feel the woods grow level,
The hare the two dogs savage is frail Man,
    The two dogs are the Pope and Devil;
And in the wind that courses through the forest,
He hears the pure truth the first angels chorused.

Odd, how his genius courts expectancy,
    And views life as a text it's read.
Yet others, seeking god in all they see,
    Not finding Him, will claim He's dead,
Or will descry false gods when history slips
Into a fraudulent Apocalypse.

This lies, however, centuries away.
    The present prospect is of hills,
The garden which he walks in, day by day,
    Leisure he restlessly fulfills,
While far below the fortress, the cascade
Drifts its cold white breath through the gorge's shade.

If everything's arranged, then even doubt
    Is simply a predestined mood;
And thus he justifies, as he works out,
    His theories and his solitude,
Gaining conviction while he frets and grieves
Till, one gray dawn in early March, he leaves.

Even this last scene's ambiguously spliced:
    The bridge creaks down, he rides across;
His mount's as humble as the mount of Christ;
    And, see, out there above the Schloss,
A widening band of chimney smoke is curled
Vaguely downwind, toward the modern world.

IN THE KING'S ROOMS

David, at Mahanaim during the Rebellion

This evening I pace chambers where I sought
To charm an old king with a shepherd's song.
Now I am king, and aging. I once thought
I could forever dwell in quiet caught
From melodies I crafted. I was wrong.

Young, loved by all, I lived beyond all doubt.
I calmed the trembling flank and frightened eye
Of the young doe—and later, led the rout
Of the invaders, lifting with a shout
The giant's head up to an answering sky.

Despised now even by my son, I raise
No shout to heaven. An uncertain friend,
A faithless leader, I can only gaze
Across a land which lent me, once, its praise
And which tonight I grudgingly defend.

Let my smooth, artful counselors secure
Victories in the name of faith and truth.
I can no longer care. Nor am I sure
Whom I should pray forgiveness for—
The old man misled or the too-favored youth.

TIMOTHY

Although the field lay cut in swaths,
Grass at the edge survived the crop:
Stiff stems, with lateral blades of leaf,
Dense cattail flower-spikes at the top.

If there was breeze and open sky,
We raked each swath into a row;
If not, we took the hay to dry
To the barn's golden-showering mow.

The hay we forked there from the truck
Was thatched resilience where it fell,
And I took pleasure in the thought
The fresh hay's name was mine as well.

Work was a soothing, rhythmic ache;
Hay stuck where skin or clothes were damp.
At length, the pick-up truck would shake
Its last stack up the barn's wood ramp.

Pumping a handpump's iron arm,
I washed myself as best I could,
Then watched the acres of the farm
Draw lengthening shadows from the wood

Across the grass, which seemed a thing
In which the lonely and concealed
Had risen from its sorrowing
And flourished in the open field.

AN AUBADE

As she is showering, I wake to see
A shine of earrings on the bedside stand,
A single yellow sheet which, over me,
Has folds as intricate as drapery
In paintings from some fine old master's hand.

The pillow which, in dozing, I embraced
Retains the salty sweetness of her skin;
I sense her smooth back, buttocks, belly, waist,
The leggy warmth which spread and gently laced
Around my legs and loins, and drew me in.

I stretch and curl about a bit and hear her
Singing among the water's hiss and race.
Gradually the early light makes clearer
The perfume bottles by the dresser's mirror,
The silver flashlight, standing on its face,

Which shares the corner of the dresser with
An ivy spilling tendrils from a cup.
And so content am I, I can forgive
Pleasure for being brief and fugitive.
I'll stretch some more, but postpone getting up

Until she finishes her shower and dries
(Now this and now that foot placed on a chair)
Her fineboned ankles, and her calves and thighs,
The pink full nipples of her breasts, and ties
Her towel up, turban-style, about her hair.

EROS

By rights one should experience holy dread
At the young woman gowned in black chiffon
Who, at a mirror, slightly turns her head,
Large eyes intent, and puts an earring on.
One should fear redwoods where the sun sinks shafts
Of glowing light through dust-revolving drafts
And where the cyclist slimly coasts through trees
As she leans forward, her arms long and brown,
And gives her brakes a moderating squeeze.

Yet the soul loves the braided rope of hair,
The sense of heat and light, the cheek's faint flush.
Time blurs; nights end; one climbs a narrow stair,
The studio's warm, the city is a hush
Of streetlamps and the snow that, all night, falls.
But later when one rises and recalls
How, in the dark, the spirit clings and melts,
It is as if the ardent, giddy rush
Had happened, somehow, to somebody else.

Gently to brush hair from the sleeping face,
To feel breath on the fingers, and to try
To check joy in that intimate, small place
Where joy's own joyousness can't satisfy—
This is pain. This is power that comes and goes.
This is as secret as the fresh clean snows
Which, destitute of traffic to confess,
Will serve at dawn as witness to a sky
Withdrawing to its high blue faultlessness.

THE LIBRARY

Emerging through the automatic doors,
I feel the Santa Anas' gusting heat.
It's five o'clock. The grainy sunlight pours
Through eucalypti whose peeled bark strips beat
The trunks to which they cling like feeble sleeves.
The campus lawns are eddyings of leaves
Viewed by day's milky, unassertive moon.
The sculpture garden has a recessed seat.
I take it, thinking of the afternoon

And of the library. Cultural oasis?
Few would object to its conserving aims.
Still, tracking books by way of data bases,
I feel I'm playing Faustian video games.
And jotting notes down from computer screens,
I doubt our armories of ways and means:
Whether in books or trusted to a disc,
The written record may, as Plato claims,
Subvert and put our memory at risk.

Yet books consoled me when I was a child,
And seeing words and software joined and sync-ed,
Even philosophers might be beguiled.
And if I relish verses nimbly linked,
Here flowing, there concluded with a twist,
It was a Greek librarian-archivist
Who had an odd pedantic inspiration—
Make prose and poems textually distinct—
And first gave lyric measures lineation.

Banners on the Art Gallery's façade
Ripple and flap; in a collegial wrath,
Two birds dispute rights to a carob pod;
A puffed-up brown bag somersaults a path
Where Rodin's *Walker* makes his headless stride.
Leaves spin up into coilings and subside.
This windy much-ado, arising from
The desert could well serve as epitaph
For Alexandria, Rome, Pergamum—

For all the ancient libraries whose collections
Have vanished in a mammoth wordless void.
And though I have the evening clouds' confections,
Thoughts of the art and science thus destroyed
Leave me a little empty and unnerved.
The consolation? Some things were preserved,
Technology now limits what is lost,
And learning, as it's presently deployed,
Is safe from any partial holocaust.

I could construct a weighty paradigm,
The Library as Mind. It's somehow truer
To recollect details of closing time.
Someone, at slotted folders on a viewer,
Tucks microfiche squares in their resting places;
Felt cloth's drawn over the exhibit cases;
The jumbled New Book Shelves are set in shape;
The day's last check-outs are thumped quickly through a
Device that neutralizes tattle-tape.

And shelvers, wheeling booktrucks through the stacks,
Switch lights off at the ends of empty aisles;
Jaded computer terminals relax;
Above lit spaces of linoleum tiles,
The hitching-forward minute hands of clocks
Hold vigil still, but a custodian locks
The main door, and the last staff members go

Home to their private lives and private trials.
Still ovenish, the Santa Anas blow

The leaves about in rustling shifting mounds;
The long, rust-colored needles pine trees shed
In broom-straw trios strew the walks and grounds;
Winding, as though along a corkscrew's thread,
A squirrel has circled down a sycamore.
The frail must, in fair times, collect and store,
And so, amid swirled papery debris,
The squirrel creeps, nosing round, compelled to hoard
By instinct, habit, and necessity.

JOSEPH

The fridge clicks, hums; light flows across
Cold sleeping tiles, and I survey
Red chilies, lime juice, tartar sauce—
Things I can't use or throw away
And which, some hours from morning, wear
An aspect of profound despair.

A glass of milk? Perhaps some food?
I draw a carton from the back.
Ranged on the wall by magnitude,
Knives gleam on their magnetic rack.
Novitiate-like, I stand before
The cylinder of white I pour.

What woke me? Was it that I sensed
The far drone of a passing plane?
I drink, then lean my head against
The chill damp of the windowpane,
And all the while the ticking clock's
Like a plain, baffling paradox.

Each quick, clenched moment's like the next.
Yet time yields shape and history.
I think—disquieted, perplexed—
How Joseph knelt at Pharaoh's knee
As he leaned from his throne to hear
The meaning of his dreams made clear

And luminous, for once, with hope.
When I look up I see in space

The moon as through a telescope:
Vague winds cross, streamingly, its face,
Remote and icy and antique,
And to its light I whisper, Speak.

SPRING EVENING

Above the baby powder clouds
The sky is china blue.
Soon, young and chattering, the crowds
Of stars come pushing through.

And this is the first dispensation,
The setting up of the odds;
This is the eve of creation,
This is the time of the gods.

APRIL WIND

—for Ann Weary

Wind, gigantic, wrestles the April leaves;
The mares are nervous, elated, tossing their manes;
We pass in file under the forest eaves
Where a magic bodarc shakes an emerald free
From each of its branched black veins;

The path is narrow, we are fingered at elbow and knee
By the grape and the cedar elm. All goes dazzling bright:
The sun has come out and now we suddenly see
How this green is the white of the plant world, the blanch
Of its secret kinship with light;

And my friend turns—the artist, who owns this ranch—
And tells how a painter will throw on a gout of white,
And feather a green glaze thereover, for a branch;
And now, strangely, we both fall silent and ride
As if we were chilled by a slight;

For through the woodland is blowing a perfume, a tide
Of sweetness from some blossoming out of our sight,
Mysterious, innocent, heavenly, known on the inside
Only, unfading; and the mares are dancing, and we,
Like disciplined riders, pull tight

On the rein and grasp with the strength of the thigh and the knee
The huge bodies that move, prehistoric and blind,
Through the now darkening glades. And we are quite free
To speak, or not, as we make for the gate we shall find
In the waves of the fragrant wind.

ON THE PAINS OF TRANSLATING
MIKLÓS RADNÓTI

*(The great Hungarian poet shot by the Nazis in 1944. His
mother and twin brother died in childbirth.)*

And now I too must wrestle with a brother
Whose dead limbs cumber me within the womb,
Whose grief I pity, but whose cord of nurture
Glides dreadful and unseen in this blind gloom.

That angel, who took Cain to be his mirror,
Knew how to die, knew how to share a grave;
Sometimes he almost overcrows my spirit,
His great feathered wings beating in the cave—

My elder brother died as I first opened
My lips in speech instead of in a scream;
Now he returns to claim the voice I borrowed,
Now he returns, the hero of my dream.

How can I share the lifeblood of our mother?
How can I let his dead voice steal my breath?
But how indeed could I deny my brother
Who, reckless, bought my birthright with his death?

For all alone among that generation
He kept the faith that I have made my name,
That ancient grace, that hard emancipation,
The love of form that touches us like flame.

What can I do but open to his service
The pulse and wordstream of the mother tongue?

Thus I subdue myself and hear him singing
Out of the land of shades where none have sung.

Could I, the Western democrat, professor,
Father, essayist, of middle age,
Be given any greater gift than this is,
To share the passion of his vassalage?

THREE SONGS

I

Much has been said of the
amorist's tendency
to see the world as a
map of her mind.
If she repines for a
lone individual,
she fills her spare time with
loving mankind.

Teeming humanity
in all its wonders, though,
when I am love-stricken,
bores me to bits.
Better to hole myself
up in a mania,
rave in a ready-made
palace of fits.

Sociable nourishment
can't hold a candle to
salving a complex and
nursing an ache.
If a big breadline forms
outside my hermitage,
I bolt the windows and
let them eat cake.

Love, say the optimists,
makes the bewitched want to
run at the masses with
spread-eagled arms.
I do not rush out, but
hoard my obsession and
crabbily contemplate
burglar alarms.

It is their orderless,
intrusive otherness
that I must keep out—this
rival, that bore.
In the ongoing film
of my own martyrdom,
real life gets left on the
cutting room floor.

Otherwise it might swoop
down on the scenery
on wings of common sense
and call my bluff,
saying, "Your passion is
test-tube-begotten, your
much-vaunted lunacy
founded on fluff."

To which (to give myself
credit) I would respond
that it was sadly but
perfectly true.
If a delirium
cannot survive without
shutting the neighbors out,
what can I do?

Only continue to
come down with symptoms and
prune the green leaves of a
fruitful despair,
hating the plotters who
peer in my hothouse and
threaten to tell me that
nothing grows there.

II

What if I locked you in my chamber,
gave you a trauma to remember?
After the days of nonstop violence
and the long nights of grisly silence,
would your rock-hard, unwilling heart
say yes, though your lips said no?

What if I shredded all your papers,
treated your past as a fuel for tapers?
Would your new name create new feelings,
or does identity have ceilings
past which a meddlesome invader
damnably cannot go?

What if I dug a moat around you,
questioned and kicked and gagged and bound you?
Solitude and interrogation
only make a capitulation
less sincere; your body may
say yes, but your mind says, no.

What if I monitored your eating,
starved your resolve with prolonged beating?
You would possess a small figure

but your big spirit would get bigger.
Oh my triumphant captive, I have
dealt you an empty blow.

Roaring pain and induced affliction
cannot make inroads on conviction;
I check your cell each hour to find you
stubbornly loath to change your mind. You
wicked dissenter, your frail bones
say yes, but your heart says no.

What if I freed you from your shackles,
shoved you outdoors with jeers and cackles?
You would soon find the wide world staler
than your vivacious, loving jailer,
but if this hell is what you think
you want, you are free to go.

III

How did you feel when you entered the church?
Left in the lurch!
What did they say when you brought back the ring?
Poor jilted thing!
Why did they laugh when they looked up its make?
It was a fake!

How did you spend your time out of town?
Tracking him down.
How did he look when you raided his room?
Pale as a groom.
What were the words the coroner used?
Vilely abused.

How many mourners can fill a hall?
Room for them all.

What are the songs the organist plays?
Dolorous lays.
What do you drop as you head for the bier?
Never a tear.

Have the embalmers earned their pay?
Pink hides the gray.
How does he look who did not survive?
Almost alive.
What does the crowd remark upon?
That he is gone!

How do you feel among these men?
Jilted again.
What do his benefactors sense?
Wasted expense!
Where is the world's most wanted dun?
Still on the run.

THREE SONGS

I

I was in the bookstore, reading the ends of mysteries,
when the gunshots went off just outside.
I was in the drugstore, seeking delicious remedies,
when the leper shuddered at my side.

In a world where love is innocent and upstanding,
sicknesses and riddles are over soon,
but when love is real, the universe starts expanding
like a crazy, out-of-control balloon.

How to know the brave new moves from the same old motions?
How to tell the first from the thirteenth prize?
By the stricken heart's obliviousness to potions,
by the awful magnitude of surprise.

II

The threnodist stopped his story in mid-sentence:
why were all the listeners looking down,
each pair of eyes encased in its own sorrow,
each pair of lips contorted in a frown?

The famous beauty entered the room expecting
a loud response, an episode of violence,
but to her great annoyance, all her suitors
stared at the walls in unprotesting silence.

Bearers of bad news would like nothing better
than to raise a purgative, public moan,
but a communal feeling is a false one:
genuine grief must run its course alone.

III

The eyes that start a fire in his head,
the heart that skips a beat for him alone,
the smiles that tingle up and down his spine
would get you somewhere if they were your own.

But someone always hovers in the room
where you and your enchanted one embrace;
look up from hot and bothered limbs to see
a jealous warden with an angel's face.

He gives you all the gorgeous words of praise
that he will give another and another,
but when he finds a phrase he really likes
he holds his tongue and saves it for his mother.

DINNER AT LE CAPRICE

How good it would be if our surroundings always
mirrored the kindest contours of our hearts,
if the unimpressive restaurant at whose table
the couple sit and stammer were named Le Caprice
and if, made braver by each successive glass
of golden potions, abetted by the kind of waiter

who looks as if he were born to be a waiter—
tall and perfectly two-toned—they promised always
to dine together; shattering all the glass
in the place with the high-pitched singing of their hearts,
pitching their flag between the camps of caprice
and earnestness, they would join hands across the table

as their feet careened and twisted under the table
to the visible astonishment of the waiter,
in whose cynical opinion what starts as caprice
ends in disaster, but who revises what he always
says when, noting their keen eyes and steadfast hearts,
he takes a photo and puts it behind glass

so that tomorrow's patrons, flicking shards of glass
at each other's throats, will look up from their table
and feel the envy blossoming in their hearts
while in the background the melancholy waiter
thinks aloud, "Love may die, but there is always
one picture-perfect couple at Le Caprice."

But pictures lie, and love is a mad caprice
doomed as fat farm animals, fragile as glass.

The worst imaginary restaurant is always
better than the suggestive carcass, the table
across whose sahara of distance we stare, and the waiter
who shakes his head at the spectacle of two hearts

as tepid and terribly ill-matched as two hearts
can be—one entertaining a bold caprice
to rush out, screaming, "Fire!", the other begging the waiter
for tips on conversation and glass after glass
of garnet poisons, and who will be at another table
the next day with the next victim, hoping as always

to do better than the glassy-eyed couple who always
come in, hearts racing, on either side of the waiter
who shows them to their table at Le Caprice.

WALTER PARMER

I

How many children must have come to pass
Beyond that door and join the long sojourn
When school bells rang the students into class

To see the world from inside out and learn
To read the words and say the magic spells
That might unlock the door for their return?

Here first they faced the guarded citadels
Of otherness, and faced the windowpane
With all it had to show them of themselves,

Strange and familiar in the standing rain,
And caught the primer's hint of mystery
When early words took shape and Jack saw Jane

And Jane looked back, as neither one would be
The same for that. But when the bell would ring
For recess, playing was its own grand prix:

The mystifying movement of the swing,
The lofty goals and races to the fence,
And basketballs more real than anything.

II

Out there the wintry playground seemed immense,
Their kitty of little words too small and blind
To make the world of sight and sound make sense,

Where at day's end one child was kept behind
To clap the powdery lessons back to chalk,
Which lingered in the wind and on the mind.

In spring they made the graduated walk
Through the elementary door and filed away,
Learning to leave as they had learned to talk.

That was the way it was, until one May
Officials put a padlock on the door
And called a final summer holiday.

In the blank stare those empty windows wore,
How lushly did the stillness seem to flower
Across a schoolyard where the neighbors swore,

Although the hands sat still in their clock tower
And the schoolhouse stood in silence, out of time,
They heard the class bells ringing on the hour.

III

On the first warm Saturday past wintertime
And through the bonfire summer into fall,
The ragweed on the fence begins to climb,

And the old boys man the court for basketball.
They pivot, dribble, juke, and sweat all day
Because they love that moment when the ball

Hangs in an arcing, flawless fadeaway
Or hits the backdoor cutter in the hands,
Some small extemporaneous display

Of grace, though every player understands
That timing falters: the jumpshot that almost
Fell in falls off, a pass skips out of bounds.

The losers leave the court; that is the cost
Of losing where a challenger appears
And winners keep on winning till they've lost.

They play a game they've played for thirty years,
Though rosters fluctuate with crossed-out names
And days turn into seasons and careers.

IV

The players were the first to notice flames
When Parmer burned. They phoned in their report
And in the sun resumed their heated games.

Along the split rail fence beyond the court,
The neighbors reconvened, whose early laughter
Welled up in tears to see the flames cavort

Across the ridge and tightrope every rafter,
To hear the building pop as windows broke,
While newsmen asked their thoughts about disaster.

The men and women cried and vaguely spoke
Of teachers, friends, and unresolved desire
That seemed just then were going up in smoke.

The rolling cameras showed the school expire
And showed the boys' apparent unconcern
As small-time Neros, backlit by a fire,

Playing along, performing in their turn,
While embers fell like autumn, red and gold,
Because the game goes on though buildings burn.

V

After a long debate, the school board sold
The brick for salvage and bulldozed the paved
Piazza where the students had enrolled.

In a vacant quarter of the yard they saved
Only the stone abutments and the arch,
Above which "Walter Parmer" was engraved.

Where parents walked a path around the park
And children rode the swings and players played,
A high school couple rolls up after dark,

Fondling through an FM serenade,
Learning another tongue and reading love
On lips that taste like gin and lemonade.

In window fog they write their names above
A steamy heart of hot and vagabond
Devotions, while that distant figure of

An oracle seems ready to respond
With secret wisdom, waiting on a word,
Opening out to nowhere but beyond.

VI

Back on the court the clatter of voices blurred
And blew away. A young man stands before
That arch, a ball on his hip. Something stirred,

He thinks, like shoes scuffing a wooden floor.
And then a chalk stick squeaks across clean slate,
Like a dry hinge turning. Down the hall a door

Is opening on a room where a classmate
Is looking at a warping windowpane,
Whose standing streams appear to corrugate

Both field and grass, and looking through the rain
He dreams a summer day and takes good aim
To see the ball go in again and again.

Then voices call the fellow to his game.
The schoolhouse vanishes. His team is on,
And he turns back to leave the way he came.

Only the arch remains, something like dawn,
An empty doorway on the open grass,
Standing for going, as well as having gone.

THE COUNTERFEITER

When he was starting out, still green,
He used to make a signature mistake
So that his hidden talent could be seen,
Reversing the flag above the White House roof.
It made him feel ingenious and aloof
To signify his forgeries as fake.

He always liked his jokes, but they are private.
Sometimes, when he is pressed about his trade,
He answers with a shrug, "I draw a profit"
Or "I trust in God." Nobody ever laughs.
In the den, above two ebony giraffes,
Hangs the first dollar that he ever made.

But making money is an enterprise
Of tedious, grave concerns. To reproduce
These symboled reproductions, his hands and eyes
Must settle on what others merely see,
The couples, columns and the Model T,
And all the framework, intricate, abstruse,

And difficult to copy by design,
With fine acanthuses and cycloid nets.
He must account for every tiny line
To duplicate the sad and distant stare
Beneath the breaking waves of Jackson's hair,
If he would tender these to pay his debts.

He has invested his adult career
In being perfect when he goes to press,

An artistry both humble and severe.
Down at the basement desk, long hours pass
With a burin and a magnifying glass.
No one suspects his notable success.

He profits by his anonymity,
But deep regret competes with honest pride:
To labor toward complete obscurity
And treasure a craft that will efface his will,
Render his name unknown and all his skill
Unrecognized, long after he has died.

WATERFALL

In still transparency, the water pools
    High in a mountain stream, then spills
Over the lip and in a sheet cascades
Across the shoal, obeying hidden rules,
      So that the pleats and braids,
The feather-stitched white water, little rills
    And divots seem to ride in place
    Above the crevices and sills,
Although the water runs along the race.

What makes these rapids, this little waterfall,
    Cascading like a chandelier
Of frosted glass or like a willow tree,
Is not the water only nor the fall
      But some complicity
Of both, so that these similes appear
    Inaccurate and limited,
    Neglecting that the bed will steer
The water as the water steers the bed.

So too with language, so even with this verse.
    From a pool of syllables, words hover
With rich potential, then spill across the lip
And riffle down the page, for better or worse,
      Making their chancy trip,
Becoming sentences as they discover
    (Now flowing, now seeming to stammer)
    Their English channels, trickling over
The periodic pauses of its grammar.

ANNUAL RETURNS

If money grew on trees,
How happy we'd be then,
The children rolling in dough,
The fathers raking it in.

With holdings in the branches
Showing a big return,
The trees would drop a fortune,
We'd all have money to burn.

As autumn leaves, however,
We find the poor still poor.
The falling stocks in trees
Are swept away from the door.

So what became of the boy
Whom teachers had to scold,
Who stared and stared out windows
Into the lands of gold,

Where after school he spent
His lonely afternoons
And shuffled home knee-deep
In rubies and doubloons?

He listens to the leaves
That rattle in a squall,
Still dreaming of a world
That profits from the fall.

Index of Forms

Anacreontic

R. S. Gwynn, "Anacreontic"

Ballad

Dana Gioia, "Summer Storm"
Marilyn Nelson, "Ballad of Aunt Geneva"
Wyatt Prunty, "To Be Sung on the Fourth of July"

Ballade

Tom Disch, "Ballade of the New God"

Blank Verse

Rafael Campo, "For J.W.," "Allegory"
Dana Gioia, "Counting the Children"
Emily Grosholz, "On the Ferry, Toward Patras," "Remembering the
    Ardèche," "The Outer Banks," "Back Trouble," "Life of a
    Salesman," "Eden"
Rachel Hadas, "Sentimental Education"
Andrew Hudgins, "Saints and Strangers," "The Hereafter," "Dead
    Christ," "Praying Drunk," "Two Ember Days in Alabama," "The
    Telling"
Paul Lake, "Blue Jay"
Sydney Lea, "The Feud," "At the Flyfisher's Shack"
Mary Jo Salter, "Frost at Midnight"

Couplet

Julia Alvarez, "How I Learned to Sweep"
Rafael Campo, "Aunt Toni's Heart"
Tom Disch, "Zewhyexary"
Frederick Feirstein, "Mark Stern Wakes Up"
R. S. Gwynn, "The Drive-In"
Marilyn Hacker, "Elysian Fields"
Rachel Hadas, "The Red Hat"
Paul Lake, "Crime and Punishment"
Sydney Lea, "Telescope"
Charles Martin, "Victoria's Secret"
Rachel Wetzsteon, "Three Songs" (first sequence, song #3)

Curtal Sonnet

R. S. Gwynn, "Release"
Wyatt Prunty, "Insomnia"
Mary Jo Salter, "Summer 1983"

Double Dactyls

Rachel Wetzsteon, "Three Songs" (first sequence, #1)

Double Sonnet

Molly Peacock, "The Wheel"

Exploded Sonnet

Molly Peacock, "Those Paperweights with Snow Inside," "The Return"

Fugue

Dana Gioia, "Lives of the Great Composers"

Hudibrastics

R. S. Gwynn, "The Drive-In"

Octet

R. S. Gwynn, "Anacreontic"
Sydney Lea, "Insomnia: The Distances"
Brad Leithauser, "The Haunted"

Quatrain

Elizabeth Alexander, "Who I Think You Are," "Deadwood Dick,"
    "Letter: Blues"
Bruce Bawer, "Grand Central Station, 20 December 1987"
Rafael Campo, "El Día de los Muertos"
Dana Gioia, "Guide to the Other Gallery"
Emily Grosholz, "Life of a Salesman"
R. S. Gwynn, "Among Philistines," "Approaching a Significant Birthday,
    He Peruses *The Norton Anthology of Poetry*"
Marilyn Hacker, "Nights of 1964-1966: The Old Reliable," "Rune of the
    Finland Woman"
Rachel Hadas, "Journey Out"
Paul Lake, "Introduction to Poetry"
Sydney Lea, "The Feud," "The Wrong Way Will Haunt You"

Brad Leithauser, "Old Bachelor Brother"
Phillis Levin, "A Meeting of Friends," "The Lost Bee," "Night Coach"
Charles Martin, "Satyr, Cunnilinguent: To Herman Melville," "Speech Against Stone," "Metaphor of Grass in California"
Molly Peacock, "How I Come to You," "Dream Come True," "Have You Ever Faked an Orgasm?"
Wyatt Prunty, "A Winter's Tale," "Elderly Lady Crossing on Green," "A Note of Thanks," "Reading Before We Read, Horoscope and Weather"
Mary Jo Salter, "Welcome to Hiroshima"
Timothy Steele, "Timothy"
Frederick Turner, "Spring Evening," "On the Pains of Translating Miklós Radnóti"
Rachel Wetzsteon, "Three Songs" (second series)
Greg Williamson, "Annual Returns"

Quintet

Bruce Bawer, "On Leaving the Artist's Colony"
Rafael Campo, "For J. W.," "Allegory"
Emily Grosholz, "Eden"
Timothy Steele, "In the King's Rooms," "An Aubade"
Frederick Turner, "April Wind"

Sapphics

Marilyn Hacker, "Elevens"

Septet

Rafael Campo, "Aunt Toni's Heart"
Charles Martin, "E.S.L"

Sestet

Tom Disch, "Convalescing in London," "The Clouds"
Frederick Feirstein, "The Rune-Maker"
R. S. Gwynn, "The Classroom at the Mall"
Wyatt Prunty, "The Ferris Wheel"
Timothy Steele, "The Wartburg, 1521-22," "Joseph"
Rachel Wetzsteon, "Three Songs" (first series, song #2)
Greg Williamson, "The Counterfeiter"

Sestina

Dana Gioia, "My Confessional Sestina"
Rachel Wetzsteon, "Dinner at Le Caprice"

Sonnet

Julia Alvarez, "*from* 33"
Bruce Bawer, "The View from an Airplane at Night, Over California"
Tom Disch, "A Bookmark"
Emily Grosholz, "The Old Fisherman"
R. S. Gwynn, "Body Bags"
Marilyn Hacker, "Did you love well what very soon you left?," "Cancer Winter"
Rachel Hadas, "Moments of Summer"
Brad Leithauser, "Post-Coitum Tristesse: A Sonnet"
Charles Martin, "Sharks at the New York Aquarium," "Easter Sunday, 1985"
Marilyn Nelson, "Balance" and "Chopin"
Molly Peacock, "Desire"

Tercet

Dana Gioia, "Counting the Children"
Rachel Hadas, "Three Silences"
Sydney Lea, "Clouded Evening, Late September"
Phillis Levin, "The Shadow Returns"
Greg Williamson, "Walter Parmer"

Terza Rima

Greg Williamson, "Walter Parmer"

Triolet

Dana Gioia, "The Country Wife"

Villanelle

Julia Alvarez, "Woman's Work"
Tom Disch, "Entropic Villanelle" and "The Rapist's Villanelle"
Marilyn Hacker, "Wagers" (elongated form)

Key to the Poems

Elizabeth Alexander

Who I Think You Are: *envelope quatrains, trochaic pentameter*
Deadwood Dick: *quatrains, xaxa pararhymes, ballad meter*
Letter: Blues: *couplet quatrains, iambic pentameter*

Julia Alvarez

How I Learned to Sweep: *couplets, tetrameter*
Woman's Work: *villanelle*
from 33: *hybrid sonnets*

Bruce Bawer

View from an Airplane at Night over California: *English sonnet*
On Leaving the Artist's Colony: *quintets, irregular rhyme, iambic pentameter*
Grand Central Station, 20 December 1987: *envelope quatrains, iambic pentameter*

Rafael Campo

For J.W.: *quintets, blank verse*
Aunt Toni's Heart: *septets, couplets, iambic pentameter*
Allegory: *quintets, blank verse*
El Día de los Muertos: *alternating quatrains, iambic pentameter*

Tom Disch

Entropic Villanelle: *villanelle, iambic tetrameter*
The Rapist's Villanelle: *villanelle, iambic pentameter*
Convalescing in London: *sestets, irregular rhyme and meter*
Zewhyexary : *couplets, anapestic tetrameter*
A Bookmark: *English sonnet*
The Clouds: *sestets, unique rhyme scheme in each stanza, iambic pentameter*
Ballade of the New God: *ballade, iambic tetrameter*

Frederick Feirstein

The Rune-Maker: *sestets, ababab rhyme scheme, iambic trimeter*
Mark Stern Wakes Up: *couplets, iambic pentameter*
Mark Stern: *irregular rhyme scheme, iambic pentameter*

Dana Gioia

Lives of the Great Composers: *fugue, iambic pentameter*
The Country Wife: *double triolet*
Counting the Children: *tercets, blank verse*
Guide to the Other Gallery: *alternating quatrains, iambic tetrameter*
Maze Without a Minotaur: *unrhymed tetrameter*
My Confessional Sestina: *sestina, pentameter*
Summer Storm: *quatrains, xaxa rhyme scheme, ballad meter*

Emily Grosholz

On the Ferry, Toward Patras: *blank verse*
Remembering the Ardèche: *blank verse*
The Old Fisherman: *Italian sonnet variation*
The Outer Banks: *nine line stanzas, blank verse*
Back Trouble: *blank verse*
Life of a Salesman: *quatrains, blank verse*
Eden: *quintets, blank verse*

R.S. Gwynn

Among Philistines: *alternating quatrains, iambic pentameter*
Anacreontic: *octets, aabbabcc rhyme scheme, iambic tetrameter*
The Drive-In: *couplets, iambic tetrameter*
Approaching a Significant Birthday, He Peruses *The Norton Anthology of Poetry: alternating quatrains, iambic pentameter*
Body Bags: *Italian sonnet variations*
The Classroom at the Mall: *sestet, abccab rhyme scheme, iambic pentameter*
Release: *curtal sonnet*

Marilyn Hacker

Wagers: *elongated villanelle, iambic pentameter*
"Did you love well what very soon you left?": *Italian sonnet*
Nights of 1964-1966: The Old Reliable: *envelope quatrains, iambic pentameter*
Elevens: *quatrains, sapphics*
Rune of the Finland Woman: *quatrains, internal rhyme, pentameter*
Elysian Fields: *couplets, iambic pentameter*
Cancer Winter: *Italian sonnets*

Rachel Hadas

Journey Out: *quatrains, xaxa rhyme scheme, iambic pentameter*
Sentimental Education: *blank verse*
Moments of Summer: *nonce sonnets*

Three Silences: *tercets, aaa rhyme scheme, iambic pentameter*
The Red Hat: *couplets, iambic pentameter*

Andrew Hudgins

Saints and Strangers: *blank verse*
Dead Christ: *blank verse*
Praying Drunk: *blank verse*
Two Ember Days in Alabama: *blank verse*
Elegy for my Father, Who is not Dead: *unrhymed iambic tetrameter*
The Hereafter: *blank verse*
The Telling: *blank verse*

Paul Lake

Crime and Punishment: *couplets, iambic pentameter*
Blue Jay: *blank verse*
In Rough Weather: *irregular rhyme scheme, iambic tetrameter*
Introduction to Poetry: *alternating quatrains, iambic pentameter*

Sydney Lea

The Feud: *quatrains, blank verse*
The Wrong Way Will Haunt You: *quatrains, xaxa rhyme scheme, iambic tetrameter*
Telescope: *couplets, tetrameter*
At the Flyfisher's Shack: *irregular rhyme scheme, iambic pentameter*
Clouded Evening, Late September: *tercets, irregular rhyme scheme, iambic pentameter*
Insomnia: The Distances: *octets, rhyming abbacccd deedfffg, etc., linking last and first lines, iambic pentameter, with lines two and three of each stanza alternating as iambic dimeter or trimeter*

Brad Leithauser

Post-Coitum Tristesse: A Sonnet: *monosyllabic sonnet*
The Haunted: *octets, xaxaxbxb rhyme scheme, anapestic and dactylic dimeter*
The Ghost of a Ghost: *irregular rhyme scheme, iambic trimeter and tetrameter*
Old Bachelor Brother: *alternating quatrains, iambic pentameter*

Phillis Levin

The Shadow Returns: *tercets, irregular rhyme scheme, tetrameter*
A Meeting of Friends: *quatrains, xaxa rhyme scheme, ballad meter variation*
The Lost Bee: *envelope quatrains, iambic tetrameter and pentameter*
Night Coach: *alternating, envelope, and ballad quatrains, iambic trimeter*

Charles Martin

Satyr, Cunnilinguent: To Herman Melville: *alternating quatrains, iambic trimeter*

Sharks at the New York Aquarium: *Italian sonnet variation*

Speech Against Stone: *alternating quatrains, iambic dimeter, trimeter, and pentameter*

Metaphor of Grass in California: *alternating quatrains, iambic pentameter*

E.S.L.: *septets, abbcbac rhyme scheme, iambic trimeter, tetrameter, and pentameter*

Easter Sunday, 1985: *hybrid sonnet*

Victoria's Secret: *couplets, anapest pentameter*

Marilyn Nelson

Balance: *English sonnet*

Chopin: *English sonnet*

The Ballad of Aunt Geneva: *quatrains, xaxa rhyme scheme, iambic trimeter and short meter*

Molly Peacock

Desire: *English sonnet, irregular meter*

Those Paperweights with Snow Inside: *Exploded sonnet (16 lines)*

How I Come to You: *quatrains, xaxa rhyme scheme, irregular dimeter*

Dream Come True: *couplet quatrains, irregular dimeter*

The Wheel: *double sonnet*

Have You Ever Faked an Orgasm?: *alternating and envelope quatrains, iambic pentameter*

The Return: *Exploded sonnet (16 lines)*

Wyatt Prunty

A Winter's Tale: *alternating quatrains, iambic tetrameter*

Insomnia: *curtal sonnet*

To Be Sung on the Fourth of July: *quatrains, xaxa rhyme scheme, iambic trimeter*

The Ferris Wheel: *couplet sestets, iambic trimeter, tetrameter, and pentameter*

Elderly Lady Crossing on Green: *alternating quatrains, iambic pentameter*

A Note of Thanks: *alternating quatrains, iambic pentameter*

Reading Before We Read: Horoscope and Weather: *alternating quatrains, iambic pentameter*

Mary Jo Salter

Welcome to Hiroshima: *alternating couplet and envelope quatrains, iambic pentameter*

What Women Want: *ten line stanzas, irregular rhyme scheme, iambic pentameter*
Summer 1983: *curtal sonnet*
Frost at Midnight: *blank verse*

Timothy Steele

The Wartburg, 1521-22: *Shakespearean sestets, iambic tetrameter and pentameter*
In The King's Rooms: *quintets, abaab rhyme scheme, iambic pentameter*
Timothy: *alternating quatrains, iambic tetrameter*
An Aubade: *quintets, abaab rhyme scheme, iambic pentameter*
Eros: *nine line stanzas, ababccdbd rhyme scheme, iambic pentameter*
The Library: *nine line stanzas, ababccdbd rhyme scheme, iambic pentameter*
Joseph: *Shakespearean sestets, iambic tetrameter*

Frederick Turner

Spring Evening: *alternating quatrains, common measure*
April Wind: *quintets, linking rhyme scheme, abacb, cdced, edefd, fdfcd, cgcgg, iambic
    pentameter*
On the Pains of Translating Miklós Radnóti: *alternating quatrains, iambic
    pentameter*

Rachel Wetzsteon

Three Songs:
    I—*octets, dactylic dimeter*
    II—*sestets, ababcR rhyme scheme, iambic tetrameter*
    III—*couplet sestets, dactylic dimeter and tetrameter*
Three Songs
    I—*alternating quatrains, trochaic pentameter and hexameter*
    II—*quatrains, xaxa rhyme scheme, iambic pentameter*
    III—*quatrains, xaxa rhyme scheme, iambic pentameter*
Dinner at Le Caprice: *sestina*

Greg Williamson

Walter Parmer: *terza rima*
The Counterfeiter: *sestets, abaccb rhyme scheme, iambic pentameter*
Waterfall: *nine line stanzas, abcacbdbd rhyme scheme, iambic trimeter, tetrameter,
    and pentameter*
Annual Returns: *quatrains, xaxa rhyme scheme, iambic trimeter*

Suggestions for Further Reading

Dick Allen, Expansionist Poetry: A Special Issue of *Crosscurrents: A Quarterly.* Vol. 8, no. 2, 1988.

Bruce Bawer, *Prophets and Professors.* Story Line Press, 1995.

Philip Dacey and David Jauss, eds. *Strong Measures: Contemporary American Poetry in Traditional Forms.* Harper and Row, 1986.

Ariel Dawson, "The Yuppie Poet." *AWP Newsletter.* May 1985.

Tom Disch, *The Castle of Indolence,* Picador, 1995.

Wayne Dodd, *Toward the End of the Century.* University of Iowa Press, 1992.

Frederick Feirstein, ed. (With Frederick Turner), *Expansive Poetry.* Story Line Press, 1989.

Annie Finch, ed., *A Formal Feeling Comes: Poems in Form by Contemporary Women.* Story Line Press, 1994.

—. *Beyond the New Formalism.* Story Line Press, 1997.

Dana Gioia, *Can Poetry Matter?* Graywolf Press, 1991.

Paul Lake, "Toward a Liberal Poetics." *Threepenny Review.* Winter 1988.

—. "Verse that Print Bred." *Sewanee Review.* Fall 1992.

David Lehman, ed., *Ecstatic Occasions, Expedient Forms.* Macmillan, 1987.

Brad Leithauser, "Metrical Illiteracy." *New Criterion.* January 1983.

—. "The Confinement of Free Verse." *New Criterion.* May 1987.

Keith Maillard, "The New Formalism and the Return of Prosody." *Antigonish Review.* Winter 1995.

James McCorkle, ed., *Conversant Essays: Contemporary Poets on Poetry.* Wayne State University Press, 1990.

Robert McDowell, "The Poetry Anthology." *The Hudson Review.* Winter 1990.

Robert McDowell, ed., *Poetry After Modernism.* Story Line Press, 1990.

Wade Newman, "An Interview with Frederick Turner." *Southwest Review.* Summer 1986.

Wyatt Prunty, *Fallen from the Symboled World: Precedents for the New Formalism.* Oxford, 1990.

Robert Richman, ed., *The Direction of Poetry.* Houghton Mifflin, 1988.

Ira Sadoff, "Neo Formalism: A Dangerous Nostalgia." *American Poetry Review.* January–February 1990.

Timothy Steele, *Missing Measures: Modern Poetry and the Revolt Against Meter.* University of Arkansas Press, 1990.

Frederick Turner, *Natural Classicism.* Paragon House, 1985.

Diane Wakoski, "The New Conservatism in American Poetry." *American Book Review*. May–June 1986.

David Wojahn, "'Yes, But . . . ': Some Thoughts on the New Formalism." *Crazyhorse*. Spring 1987.

Elizabeth Alexander (b. 1962) published her first collection of poems, *The Venus Hottentot*, in 1990. She was educated at Yale and Boston University, where she studied with Derek Walcott. More of her work has appeared in *The Southern Review* and other periodicals, and she has taught at the University of Chicago since 1991.

Julia Alvarez (b. 1950) is a poet and novelist who came to the United States from the Dominican Republic. Her collections of poems include *Homecoming* and *El Otro Lado/The Other Side*. She has published two novels, *How the Garcia Girls Lost Their Accents*, which won the 1991 PEN Oakland/Josephine Miles Book Award, and *In the Time of the Butterflies*. She teaches at Middlebury College.

Bruce Bawer (b. 1956) is a poet and critic who lives in New York City. His articles have appeared in *The New Criterion*, *The Wall Street Journal*, *The American Scholar*, *The Nation*, *The Hudson Review*, and many other periodicals. In addition to his collection of poems, *Coast to Coast*, he has published *The Middle Generation*, *Diminishing Fictions*, *The Aspect of Eternity*, *A Place at the Table: The Gay Individual in American Society*, and *Prophets and Professors: Essays on the Lives and Works of Modern Poets*.

Rafael Campo (b. 1964) received an M.D. from Harvard Medical School. In addition to his medical publications, he has published poetry and prose in numerous periodicals and anthologies, including *In the Company of Solitude: American Writing from the AIDS Pandemic*. A collection of poems, *The Other Man Was Me*, was a selection of the National Poetry Series in 1993 and appeared from Arte Publico Press in 1994. *The Poetry of Healing: A Doctor's Education in Empathy, Identity, and Desire* appeared from Norton, and another book is appearing from Duke University Press.

Tom Disch (b. 1940) is a prolific novelist, poet, and critic who lives in New York City. His novels include *Camp Concentration*, *334*, *The Businessman*, and *The Priest*. Among his collections of poems are *Burn This*, *Dark Verses and Light*, and *Yes, Let's*. He has also written books for children like *The Brave Little Toaster*. A collection of literary essays, *The Castle of Indolence*, was published by Picador in 1995. His criticism regularly appears in *The New York Times*, *Los Angeles Times*, *Washington Post*, *The Hudson Review*, *The Nation*, *TLS*, and elsewhere.

Frederick Feirstein (b. 1940) has had six books of poems published and eight plays produced. His first book was selected by *Choice* as one of the two Outstanding Books of poetry for 1975. His fourth and sixth books (1986 and

1995) won the *Quarterly Review of Literature*'s international competition. Feirstein has also won a Guggenheim Fellowship in poetry, the PSA's John Masefield Award, and England's Arvon prize. Story Line will publish his *New & Selected Poems* in 1997.

Dana Gioia (b. 1950) has published two collections of poems, *Daily Horoscope* and *The Gods of Winter*. He has also published a collection of his essays, *Can Poetry Matter?* and a translation of Eugenio Montale's *Motteti: Poems of Love*. He is the editor, with William Jay Smith, of *Poems from Italy*, and, with Michael Palma, of *New Italian Poets*. He has also edited Weldon Kees's *The Ceremony and Other Stories*. For fifteen years a business executive in New York, Gioia has worked as a freelance writer since 1992. His work has appeared in *The New Yorker*, *The Hudson Review*, and many other periodicals. Recently he returned with his family to his native California.

Emily Grosholz (b. 1950) is a professor of philosophy at Pennsylvania State University. She has taught at Bread Loaf and the Sewanee Writers Conference and is an advisory editor of *The Hudson Review*, where her poems and articles have often appeared. Her books of poems are *The River Painter*, *Shores and Headlands*, and *Eden*. A fourth collection, *Accident and Essence*, is forthcoming. She has received grants from the Ingram Merrill and the Guggenheim Foundations.

R. S. Gwynn (b. 1948) is the author of a number of collections of poems, including *The Drive-In*, *Body Bags*, *The Narcissiad*, and *The Area Code of God*. For several years he monitored "The Year in Poetry" for *The Dictionary of Literary Biography*. His essays, reviews, translations, and poems have also appeared in *The Sewanee Review*, *The Hudson Review*, and elsewhere. "Among Philistines" has the distinction of being the final poem chosen for inclusion in *Poetry* during the tenure of John Frederick Nims. He lives in Beaumont, Texas, and teaches at Lamar University.

Marilyn Hacker (b. 1942) has won the National Book Award, fellowships from the Guggenheim and the Ingram Merrill Foundations, and the Lamont Poetry Award from the Academy of American Poets. She is the author of *Presentation Piece*, *Separations*, *Love, Death and the Changing of the Seasons*, *Going Back to the River*, and *Winter Numbers*. Her *Selected Poems: 1965–1990* won the Poets' Prize. A former editor of *13th Moon* and *The Kenyon Review*, she lives in New York and Paris.

Rachel Hadas (b. 1948) is a poet, translator, and critic who lives in New York City and teaches at Rutgers University. She is the editor of *Unending Dialogue: Voices from an AIDS Poetry Workshop* and author of several books of poems, including *Starting from Troy*, *Slow Transparency*, *A Son from Sleep*, *Pass It On*, *Living in*

Time, Mirrors of Astonishment, and *Empty Bed.* A critical book on Robert Frost and George Seferis appeared in 1984. She has translated Seneca, Baudelaire, and other classical and modern poets.

Andrew Hudgins (b. 1951) was born in Texas and now teaches at the University of Cincinnati. He is the recipient of numerous awards, including a Wallace Stegner Fellowship at Stanford, an Alfred Hodder Fellowship at Princeton, an Academy of American Poets Award, and grants from the National Endowment for the Arts. His book-length sequence, *After the Lost War,* won the Poets' Prize. His other collections of poems include *Saints and Strangers, The Never-Ending,* and *The Glass Hammer.* A collection of his essays, *The Glass Anvil,* is forthcoming in the University of Michigan's Poets on Poetry series.

Paul Lake (b. 1951) is the author of a collection of poems, *Another Kind of Travel,* and a novel, *Among the Immortals.* A second poetry collection, *Walking Backward,* has recently appeared from Story Line Press, and he is at work on another novel. His essays, poems, and stories have appeared in many periodicals, including *Threepenny Review, AWP Newsletter,* and *The Paris Review.* He teaches at Arkansas Technical University in Russellville.

Sydney Lea (b. 1942), founder and former editor of *The New England Review,* is the author of poetry, fiction, and essays. His collections of poetry include *Searching the Drowned Man, The Floating Candles, No Sign, Prayer for the Little City,* and *The Blainville Testament.* He has published a novel, *A Place in Mind,* and a book of naturalist essays and meditations, *Hunting the Whole Way Home.* A fellow of the Guggenheim Foundation and the Bellagio Center, he has taught at Dartmouth and Middlebury Colleges and in Italy. A volume of his selected poems is forthcoming from the University of Illinois Press. He lives in Newbury, Vermont.

Brad Leithauser (b. 1953) is a novelist, poet, and critic, and has a law degree from Harvard. The winner of a MacArthur Fellowship and numerous poetry prizes, he currently lives in Massachusetts with his wife, the poet Mary Jo Salter, and their two daughters. His collections of verse are *Hundreds of Fireflies, Cats of the Temple,* and *The Mail from Anywhere.* His novels include *Equal Distance* and *Hence.* His essays have appeared in *The New Yorker, The New Criterion, The New York Review of Books,* and many other periodicals.

Phillis Levin (b. 1954), Senior Editor of *Boulevard,* is the author of *Temples and Fields,* which won the Norma Farber First Book Award from The Poetry Society of America. She is the recipient of an Ingram Merrill Grant. Her poetry has appeared widely in magazines in the United States and abroad, including *The Paris Review, Poetry,* and *PN Review* (Great Britain). She teaches at the University of Maryland and lives in New York City.

Charles Martin (b. 1942) is a poet and translator whose books include *Room for Error, Passages from Friday,* and *Steal the Bacon.* He is also the author of a critical introduction to Catullus and a translation of the same poet. His work has appeared in *The New Yorker, The Hudson Review,* and *Poetry,* which gave him its Bess Hokin Award. He teaches at Queensborough Community College and in the Writing Seminars at Johns Hopkins University.

Marilyn Nelson (b. 1946) graduated from the University of California, Davis, and holds postgraduate degrees from the University of Pennsylvania and the University of Minnesota. Under the name Marilyn Nelson Waniek she has published *For the Body, Mama's Promises,* and *The Homeplace,* all from L.S.U. Press, and two collections of verse for children. A new collection, *Magnificat,* has also appeared from L.S.U. Press. She has received many awards for her work and is professor of English at the University of Connecticut, Storrs.

Molly Peacock (b. 1947) was born in Buffalo, New York, and now divides her time between New York City and London, Ontario. Formerly president of the Poetry Society of America, she has received fellowships from the Ingram Merrill Foundation and the NEA. Her collections of poetry are *And Live Apart, Raw Heaven, Take Heart,* and *Original Love.* Poems of hers have appeared in such magazines as *The New Yorker, The Paris Review, The Nation,* and *The New Republic.*

Wyatt Prunty (b. 1947) is a poet and critic who teaches at the University of the South, where he directs the Sewanee Writers Conference. From 1969–1972 he served in the U.S. Navy. His collections of poetry include *The Times Between, Balance as Belief, What Women Know, What Men Believe,* and *The Run of the House.* His critical book, *Fallen from the Symboled World: Precedents for the New Formalism,* was published by the Oxford University Press. His poems have appeared in *American Scholar, The New Criterion,* and *Shenandoah.* He is poetry editor of *Sewanee Theological Review.*

Mary Jo Salter (b. 1954) was once poet-in-residence at the Robert Frost Place, and later won a Discovery/The Nation Award and fellowships from the American Academy in Rome, the Guggenheim Foundation, and the NEA. She has been poetry editor of *The New Republic* and, in addition to a children's book called *The Moon Comes Home,* has published three collections of poetry: *Henry Purcell in Japan, Unfinished Painting* (a Lamont Prize winner), and *Sunday Skaters.* She lives in Massachusetts with her husband, the poet Brad Leithauser, and their two daughters.

Timothy Steele (b. 1948) grew up in Vermont and was educated at Stanford and Brandeis. His collections of poems are *Uncertainties and Rest, The Prudent Heart, Sapphics Against Anger,* and *The Color Wheel.* He has published a critical book, *Missing Measures: Modern Poetry and the Revolt Against Meter.* Among his honors are a Guggenheim Fellowship, a Peter I.B. Lavan Award from the Academy of American Poets, and a Commonwealth Club of California Medal for Poetry. He lives in Los Angeles, where he is a professor of English at California State University.

Frederick Turner (b. 1943), Founders Professor of Arts and Humanities at the University of Texas at Dallas, was born in England and grew up in Central Africa, becoming a U.S. citizen in 1977. *Shakespeare and the Nature of Time,* his Oxford dissertation, was published by Clarendon Press. He is also the author of *The New World: An Epic Poem, Natural Classicism: Essays on Literature and Science, Genesis: An Epic Poem, Rebirth of Value: Meditations on Beauty, Ecology, Religion, and Education, April Wind,* and other books. His work appears in *Poetry, Harper's,* and numerous other periodicals.

Rachel Wetzsteon (b. 1967) is the author of *The Other Stars,* a selection of the National Poetry Series in 1993 and published by Viking/Penguin in 1994. She has degrees from Yale and Johns Hopkins and is the recipient of an Ingram Merrill grant. Her poems have appeared in *The Kenyon Review, The New Republic, The Paris Review,* and many other periodicals. She was born and grew up in New York City and lives there today.

Greg Williamson (b. 1964) grew up in Nashville, Tennessee, and has received degrees from Vanderbilt University, the University of Wisconsin, and the Johns Hopkins University, where he teaches in the Writing Seminars. His poems have appeared in *Poetry, The New Republic, The Yale Review,* and other periodicals. His first book, *The Silent Partner,* was the winner of the 1995 Nicholas Roerich Poetry Prize from Story Line Press.

Notes on the Editors

Mark Jarman (b. 1952) is the author of five books of poetry, *North Sea, The Rote Walker, Far and Away, The Black Riviera,* and *Iris,* a book-length poem. Awards for his work include a Joseph Henry Jackson Award and fellowships from the National Endowment for the Arts and the John Simon Guggenheim Memorial Foundation. *The Black Riviera* won The Poets' Prize for 1991. He is a Professor of English at Vanderbilt University. *Questions for Ecclesiastes,* a new collection of his poetry, and *The Secret of Poetry,* a book of his criticism, are both forthcoming from Story Line Press.

David Mason (b. 1954) is the author of *The Buried Houses,* co-winner of the 1991 Nicholas Roerich Poetry Prize. His second collection of poems, *The Country I Remember,* contains his long title poem, which won the Alice Fay Di Castagnola Award from The Poetry Society of America, as well as twelve shorter pieces. Both books are published by Story Line Press. He is also a translator, fiction writer, and critic, whose work appears regularly in such periodicals as *The Hudson Review, Poetry, Grand Street, The Harvard Review,* and *The Sewanee Review.* Currently he is Associate Professor of English at Moorhead State University in Minnesota.